SOFTWARE PROCESS QUALITY

COMPUTER-AIDED ENGINEERING

Series Editor

Mark E. Coticchia

Carnegie Mellon University
Pittsburgh, Pennsylvania

ADDITIONAL VOLUMES IN PREPARATION

SOFTWARE PROCESS QUALITY

Management and Control

RON S. KENETT
KPA Ltd. and
Tel Aviv University
Herzlia Pituah, Israel

EMANUEL R. BAKER
Software Engineering Consultants, Inc.
Los Angeles, California

MARCEL DEKKER, INC.   NEW YORK · BASEL

ISBN: 0-8247-1733-3

This book is printed on acid-free paper.

Headquarters
Marcel Dekker, Inc.
270 Madison Avenue, New York, NY 10016
tel: 212-696-9000; fax: 212-685-4540

Eastern Hemisphere Distribution
Marcel Dekker AG
Hutgasse 4, Postfach 812, CH-4001 Basel, Switzerland
tel: 44-61-261-8482; fax: 44-61-261-8896

World Wide Web
http://www.dekker.com

The publisher offers discounts on this book when ordered in bulk quantities.
For more information, write to Special Sales/Professional Marketing at the
headquarters address above.

Current printing (last digit):
10 9 8 7 6 5 4 3 2

PRINTED IN THE UNITED STATES OF AMERICA

To the memory of my parents and father-in-law, Raymonde and Aby Kenett and Yechiel Steiner, and to my special mother-in-law, Frida Steiner, who are my links to the past and created the present and the future.

To my wife, Sima, to my daughter and son-in-law, Dolav and Nir, and to my three sons, Ariel, Dror, and Yoed. They have all contributed, in many ways, to this book.

RSK

I would like to dedicate this book to the memory of my parents, Rabbi Morris and Yetta Baker, who taught me (among other things) the virtues of diligence, study, and hard work. I would also like to dedicate this to my wife, Judy, my sons, Todd and Russ, and my daughter-in-law, Heidi, who share in this accomplishment.

ERB

Series Introduction

The Computer-Aided Engineering series represents a commitment by Marcel Dekker, Inc., to develop a book program with the goal of providing the most current information in a form easily accessible to practitioners, educators, and students. Titles in the series include works focused on specific technologies, as well as more comprehensive texts and reference books. All titles will present fundamental principles along with the latest methodologies.

The term computer-aided engineering (CAE) has widespread meaning throughout engineering disciplines as well as for this series. The series encompasses all computer-based applications used in design, manufacturing, and analysis. Various computer platforms, hardware configurations, and software programs are addressed, along with the trends, industries, and state-of-the-art applications. The overriding emphasis is on the use of computer technology as related to current engineering processes, methods, and tools.

Computer-aided engineering is a science and technology of great significance and is fundamental to total quality. It generally is faster, less expensive, and more precise than the conventional "test and build" approach. CAE provides commercial organizations with a competitive advantage, resulting in less product development time and cost and offering alternatives that could not be considered in the past. Considering the competitiveness in which engineering operates in today's world, business without this technology will not survive in the long term.

Mark E. Coticchia

Foreword

Software quality is seen by many as a mysterious topic.

No one who has experienced the consequences of bad software doubts the importance of quality in software. Yet, of all the "mysteries" of producing software, none are more obscure than those relating to quality. As a result, software quality is often seen as an elusive and mysterious subject, perhaps the most ignored topic in the world of software development as well as in the realm of research and education.

Actually, "mystery" is the wrong word to describe how many people seem to view the subject of software quality. "Myth" might be a better term. Just as almost everyone knows what quality is (or, so they think), most people hold certain beliefs about how it is achieved. The problem is that many of those beliefs about how one can obtain software quality are false.

Probably the most prevalent myth is that, while quality is important, delivering something *now* is essential. Following closely in popularity are various fallacies, including:

> Quality is the responsibility of someone else, not me.
> We will add it in the next release.
> It is a technical problem that the programmers must deal with.
> If we just had better development tools, people, or management, we wouldn't have a quality problem.
> We need to add a quality inspection function.

Kenett and Baker, in this highly pragmatic book that is also well-grounded in theory, go a long way toward exposing these myths for what they are and providing correct principles with which to replace them. They bring a rare blend of extensive experience, deep study, and broad domain of application to the topic.

The authors' key idea is completely in line with well-proven theories and the experience of the best developers of quality software. While quality is in the eye of the beholder, we nonetheless can define it for any specific piece of software and achieve it by devising an appropriate system of processes that shapes what happens as we move from concept to delivered system through continual enhancement and change.

Although I have tried for many years to help managers and technical developers improve the quality of their software processes—and thus of the resulting software—and I learned a good deal from this book about achieving quality software. I know that you will, too.

> Peter A. Freeman, Ph.D.
> Dean and Professor
> College of Computing
> Georgia Institute of Technology
> Atlanta, Georgia

Preface

Software presents both an opportunity and a threat. Software runs our lives. The list of applications in which software is a critical component is endless: elevators, airlines, telecommunications, medical devices, education, and countless others. Data from the Software Engineering Institute indicates that approximately 60% of software development organizations that have had formal assessments designed to determine how their software is developed are at the lowest level of capability. These assessments are based on the Capability Maturity Model—a framework for achieving process improvement. This lowest level is characterized as ad hoc and chaotic, having virtually nothing in the way of organized project management or software engineering practices. Over 600 organizations worldwide have gone through such assessments. These are organizations that have either embarked on improvement efforts of their software development process or made a commitment to do so. If we add in all the organizations that have not had assessments performed, or have no plans to implement process improvement, we estimate that the number of organizations at the lowest level is probably well in excess of 80%.

What is the consequence of this low level of process capability operating in most organizations developing software? Let's look at personal computers. How many users are really happy with the quality of their software products? Horror stories about people losing hours of work because the computer locked up at an inopportune time are common topics of conversations in social and business meetings. What about mainframe software? Newspapers frequently describe how bugs in telephone switching software cause catastrophic outages, or how bank information systems lose track of millions of dollars in accounts.

Processes are the link between past, present, and future activities. We believe that following a highly capable process does make a difference. Achieving such process capability requires continuous improvement.

What are the barriers to process improvement? A nonexhaustive list includes:

Lack of data: Many organizations have no idea what their current levels of performance are. They have never implemented effective measurement programs, and have very little idea whether they are performing well or are in deep trouble. For instance, they do not know if the bug rate in their delivered software is at, above, or below industry norms, or how long it really takes to deliver a given set of capabilities. For many companies that do collect data, the data is never used, or is not used properly.

Extreme focus on time to market: Working on process improvement is perceived as getting in the way of getting new products (or updates to existing products) out the door. Some companies feel that, while process improvement would be nice to have, they just can't spare the people or the time.

Cost: While there is often money to acquire new tools or computing equipment, there is usually little money allocated to process improvement. It's not perceived as something that requires a capital investment.

Managers who don't understand process: Many people can recognize the importance of process in activities such as car manufacturing or chemical processing, but don't recognize the fact that it plays an important role in software and hardware development. Many software development organizations are populated with "developers" who know how to hack out code under extreme time pressure, but have never had the opportunity to work in an environment in which development was focused upon quality. These people later become software project leaders or software development managers. Why would they require their developers to follow a process as managers when they never followed one as developers?

The educational pipeline: Virtually no schools teach software engineering as an undergraduate program. Few computer science programs teach this curriculum from the perspective of a development cycle process. Any appreciation of the value of process is picked up along the way through experience.

Passive management: Many senior managers who decide to implement process improvement believe that it can be done by "decree." They often do not hold their middle managers accountable for the success or failure of process improvement. Many manage process improvement by "remote control". The middle managers, in many instances, are like kamikaze pilots with several targets to hit, all at once.

Undoubtedly, there are other factors, as well, that get in the way of effective process improvement. But process improvement doesn't have to be so hard. Process improvement can be implemented and managed effectively. It takes careful planning and monitoring, but it can be done. *SOFTWARE PROCESS QUALITY: Management and Control* presents a methodology for establishing the current status of a software development process and laying out a reasoned plan for process improvement. The book identifies practical ways of implementing measurement programs used to establish current levels of performance and baselines against which to measure achieved improvements.

The book provides details and examples of measures and metrics that can be used to establish a baseline, as well as for use in monitoring process improvement projects. The book concludes with a realistic case study to illustrate how all the methods, tools and techniques discussed in the book fit together.

SOFTWARE PROCESS QUALITY: Management and Control was designed to be practical but not necessarily exhaustive. Our objective was to provide the reader with a workable approach for achieving cost-effective process improvement.

Professor Gideon Langholz of Tel Aviv University's School of Engineering, who convinced the first author, in 1983, to design a graduate course on software reliability, planted the seed for this book. The course grew in popularity and is now entitled "Quantitative Methods in Software Development." Many thanks are due Professor Langholtz for his vision, ongoing support, and friendship. Finally, we would like to thank Russell Dekker and Brian Black and all the people at Marcel Dekker, Inc., associated with this book for their patience. This book has been in work for some time, and they never gave up on us.

Ron S. Kenett
Emanuel R. Baker

Contents

1
A Framework for Software Quality*

1.1 INTRODUCTION

Quality, in some respects, is an elusive characteristic—not because it is difficult to achieve (once we decide what it is), but because it is difficult to describe. A universally accepted and commonly understood definition is difficult to achieve. The relationship between quality and the factors that affect it is even more complex to describe. Consequently, when two people are discussing "quality," they are often talking about different things.

In order to establish a frame of reference for the concepts in this book, a definition of quality and a description of the factors affecting it are necessary. This introductory chapter sets the stage by providing our definition and our concept of the relationship between quality and its influencing factors.

The relationship between the quality of a software product and the organization responsible for producing it is multi-faceted. This relationship depends upon many factors, including the business strategy and business structure of the organization, available talent, and the processes and resources used to produce the product. The processes, which are of particular concern, consist of the development activities selected and implemented by the organization to attain the product quality desired.

---

* Adapted from Chapter 4, "Software Quality Program Organization," *Handbook of Software Quality Assurance*, 2nd edition, G. Gordon Schulmeyer and James I. McManus, eds., Van Nostrand Reinhold, New York, 1992.

To better understand the significance of these relationships, let's consider the following precepts. First, consider our definition of software quality. Software quality is defined as, "The degree to which a software product possesses a specified set of attributes necessary to fulfill a stated purpose" [1]. If we dig beneath the surface of this definition, the following points become apparent.

- A large number of the project personnel are involved in implementing the requirements (i.e., impacting the "degree to which [the] software product possesses [the] specified set of attributes").
- Some of the project personnel are (or should be) involved in explicitly defining the project requirements (i.e., defining the "stated purpose" and the corresponding "set of attributes necessary to fulfill" it).
- Some more of the project personnel are (or should be) involved in determining how well the requirements have been met (i.e., determining the "degree to which [the] software product possesses [the] specified set of attributes"). These personnel are the testers, software quality assurance (SQA) personnel, and other personnel involved in performing software product and process quality evaluations.
- Another group of project personnel are (or should be) involved in performing control functions to ensure that inadvertent actions don't result in a degradation of the quality that has already been built into the software. These personnel are project leaders, configuration management (CM) staff, and SQA personnel.

What emerges from this description is the fundamental and well-known principle that "Quality is everybody's business." As can be seen, virtually everyone working on a project affects the quality of the software product in some way; however, only those producing the product actually build the quality into it. When we consider how software development projects are organized, this translates to: "Quality is affected by many, but effected by few." Because of this, the ultimate responsibility for the quality of the software product lies with management: line and project management. It is management's responsibility to integrate the efforts of "the many" and "the few" and bring them to bear on the development or maintenance effort to accomplish the quality objectives.

Secondly, there is a method for structuring projects and organizations to control the product quality, and that is to implement a software quality program (SQP). The SQP has three critical elements, each of which will be described below. Each of these elements spawns a series of tasks, each of which has some impact on the quality of the software product. Management must determine the allocation of these tasks and assign them to the available personnel or organizations supporting the project, express them in a SQP plan, and obtain the commitment of the supporting organizations. The SQP plan may be a separate plan or may be an integral part of the software development plan (e.g., the software project management plan).

1.2 SOFTWARE QUALITY PROGRAM

The software quality program is the overall approach to influence and determine the level of quality achieved in a software product. It consists of the activities necessary to:

- Establish requirements for the quality of a software product.
- Establish, implement, and enforce methodologies, processes and procedures to develop, operate, and maintain the software.
- Establish and implement methodologies, processes, and procedures to evaluate the quality of a software product and to evaluate associated documentation, processes, and activities that impact the quality of the product.

Figure 1.1 illustrates the elements of the SQP.

The foundation of the software quality program is not how well one can measure product quality nor the degree to which one can assess product quality. While these are essential activities, they alone will not attain the specified quality. Quality can only be built in during the development process. Software quality cannot be tested, audited, evaluated, measured, or inspected into the product. This is a concept that is not well understood by many software development organizations, whether they are organizations that develop software for sale, develop software only for in-house use, or develop software under a contractual arrangement. Furthermore, it is not

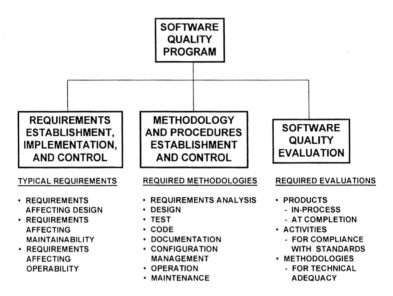

Figure 1.1 Software quality elements.

sufficient to pay attention to only the development aspects of the software enterprise. Once the quality has been built in, the operating and maintenance processes must not degrade it. It is that understanding that is the basis for the software quality program.

The foundation of the SQP stems from the definition of software quality. It is the concept that product quality means, in effect, achieving its intended end use, as defined by the user or customer. Does the software do what it is supposed to do? In other words, does it correctly meet requirements that accurately capture what the user or customer wants? These requirements include the software functional and performance requirements, and also include requirements for maintainability, portability, interoperability, and so on. The significance of this concept is that product requirements are, in reality, the quality requirements. And they must *accurately* capture and reflect the way that the user/customer wants to use the software.

Figure 1.2 illustrates the elements of the software quality program and how it affects software quality. The interaction of the SQP with the other parts of the project elements, as depicted in the figure,

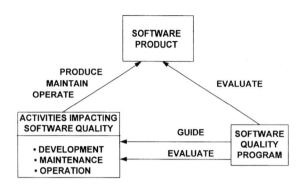

Figure 1.2   What creates quality software?

is necessarily complex. That involvement is at all levels of the project organization and takes place throughout the project's life. In some cases, the SQP directs the other activities; in other circumstances, it can only influence those activities. In any case, all the project activities, in some way, affect software product quality.

The software quality program includes both technical and management activities. For instance, if we look at the element of the SQP concerned with methodologies for software development, enforcing these methodologies (in order to build quality into the software) is a management activity, while the specification of the methodologies is a technical activity.

1.2.1   Requirements Management

The first element of the software quality program is concerned with the establishment of the requirements for the software to be produced on a project. These include the processing requirements as well as the requirements for the design of the databases. Processing requirements, as used here, refer to the functional, performance, security, safety, "ility" (i.e., reliability, maintainability, characteristics), and other related attributes that the software should possess.

As previously pointed out, the requirements for the software are, in fact, the requirements for the quality of the software. Consequently, the requirements must accurately reflect the functionality, performance, etc., that the customer or user expects to see in the software.

This activity includes not only defining the requirements but also baselining (formalizing) them, as well. This means that once the definition of the requirements are reasonably stable, they must be formally documented and placed under the control of a centralized authority. They should not be changed by any individual acting alone, but, rather, should be changed only after representatives of other applications that interface with the application for which the change is contemplated concur that (1) there is no impact on them, or (2) if there is an impact, that it is acceptable. [For a more detailed discussion of the mechanics of software configuration management, see Reference 2]. However, merely defining and formalizing the requirements is insufficient. The requirements must be enforced. The developers must not be allowed to ignore them or unilaterally deviate from them. This can often occur. No developer can assume that he or she is better qualified than the customer or the user to know what is needed. Such assumptions can often lead to the production of software that doesn't meet customer needs. Intentional deviation may not always cause significant problems (see Reference 3), but the potential is clearly there.

The process of defining and establishing the requirements and controlling changes to them involves interfaces with the other two elements of the SQP: establishment of methodologies and quality evaluation. Two kinds of interfaces with the establishment of methodologies exist. One is the specification of the preferred methodology or methodologies for performing requirements analysis. In order to ensure consistency in the quality of the requirements and uniformity in the way that they are documented, the methodologies must be institutionalized. That is, there must be a common way of performing requirements analysis within each project—one that is well understood and practiced by all the affected developers. For example, a project's use of data flow or object oriented analysis to define requirements results from the establishment of one or the other as the preferred methodology for performing requirements analysis.

The second interface has to do with baselining requirements and controlling changes to them. This process, or methodology, is known as a "configuration management process." This is a management methodology implemented to:

- Prevent uncontrolled changes to baselined items
- Improve the likelihood that the development effort will re-

sult in quality software, and that software maintenance will
not degrade it

The discipline of configuration management assists project management in ensuring that the requirements will be managed and controlled.

The interface between this element of the SQP and the software
quality evaluation element is concerned with the evaluation of the
requirements. They must be correct, complete, understandable, test-
able, and feasible (among other features). They must also correctly
capture the user's needs. As pointed out in Reference 3, total compliance with requirements does not guarantee quality software. If the
user's needs have not been properly captured, errors exist in the requirements. Compliance with requirements will then produce software that does not satisfy the intended end use. Clearly, requirements must be evaluated for adequacy with respect to all aspects
while they evolve and develop.

1.2.2 Methodology Establishment and Implementation

The second element of the SQP pertains to the establishment, implementation, and enforcement of methodologies for the development,
operation, and maintenance activities for the software product.
These are the processes by which the software will be developed,
operated, and maintained.

There is a very strong link between software quality and the
processes used to develop it. If the processes in use by a software
development organization are not well defined or organized, the
quality of their software products will not be predictable or repeatable from project to project. The dependency of software quality on
processes has been characterized by the Software Engineering Institute (SEI) at Carnegie Mellon University in a Capability Maturity
Model^{SM} (CMM)* [4–6]. Five levels of maturity are described by the
CMM. The levels, their names, and the characteristics which describe when the organization has reached that level are identified
below:

---

* The Capability Maturity Model (CMM) is a service mark of the Software
Engineering Institute.

- Level 1: *Initial*: Chaotic, ad hoc; organized practices do not exist for a consistent project management discipline—nor do any exist for performing a consistent software development process.
- Level 2: *Repeatable*: Development process is intuitive, rather than codified; procedures for project planning and management, SCM, SQA, requirements management, and subcontractor management exist and are implemented. Success on development projects, however, is very much dependent on key individuals, and not on process. In times of crisis, established procedures are abandoned.
- Level 3: *Defined*: A process focus exists in the organization. A Software Engineering Process Group (SEPG) exists and is charged with that responsibility. Software development and project management processes are codified and followed for all projects. Procedures and tools for software development exist and are implemented. When faced with a crisis, the organization continues to use the defined process.
- Level 4: *Managed*: Minimum basic process measurements have been established. A process data base and the resources to manage it have also been established. Resources to gather and maintain the data have been established. Process measures are used to identify when processes have gone awry and to implement corrective actions. Quantitative measures for product quality have been defined and implemented.
- Level 5: *Optimizing*: Process measures are being collected and entered into the process data base. The process data base is being used to fine tune and optimize the development and maintenance processes. The process measures are utilized to evaluate candidate new technologies for implementation in the process.

A methodology, called the software process assessment (SPA), has been developed by the SEI to determine the capability level at which software development organizations are functioning [7,8]. The original SPA methodology was based on an older "process maturity model" [4,17]. The process maturity model was not as robust as the CMM, and did not have the detailed structure contained in it (see Chapter 3 for a discussion of the structure). This prompted the development of the CMM (which, in its preliminary form, was referred to as Version 1.0), and an upgraded assessment methodology. The released version of the CMM was identified as Version 1.1. When Version 1.1 of the CMM was released, the SPA methodology was upgraded, and renamed. It is now called a "CMM-Based Appraisal for Internal Process Improvement (CBA-IPI)." It is still sometimes loosely referred to as a SPA or an assessment.

As of October, 1997, 606 organizations have had assessments performed. This total includes assessments performed under the original SPA methodology, as well as CBA-IPIs. Of these organizations, 59.4% were found to be functioning at Level 1, 24.3% at Level 2, 13.9% at Level 3, 2.1% at Level 4, and 0.3% at Level 5 [9]. Based on the definitions of the levels of the CMM, 88.6% of the organizations surveyed do not have well-established, codified software development processes.

These figures do not represent a random sampling of the software industry. They are the recorded result of assessments willingly undertaken by organizations who have decided to embark on a process improvement program. There are many who believe that if a true random sample were taken, the number of organizations at Level 1 would be much higher (perhaps upward of 75% or greater) and, correspondingly, the number at the higher levels would be fewer. If we accept the premise that the quality of a software product is dependent on the quality of the process used to develop it, then the logical conclusion is that the consistent production of quality software is a sometime thing for the vast majority of software development organizations.

Data gleaned from various sources indicate that the Japanese software industry is achieving defect rates two orders of magnitude better than those of the "best in class" U.S. companies [10]. A reason why the Japanese are achieving such low defect rates, based on reviews of the Japanese software industry conducted in 1984 and 1989, is because of their emphasis on understanding and improving the software development process. The same reports also indicate the authors' beliefs that many of the Japanese companies are operating at Levels 3, 4, and 5, whereas 16.3% of U.S. companies are operating at Level 3 and above, based on the October 1997 figures.

There is a great deal of interest in the CMM within India, and a number of commercial organizations have set off on efforts to achieve Level 3. A significant number of Indian software organizations have had software process assessments performed. In fact, one of the very few organizations operating at Level 5, although not specifically identified in Reference 9, is a Motorola operation in India [18]. Indian software development organizations have frequently been selected as subcontractors by U.S. companies because of their low cost and reputation for high quality.

From the foregoing, it can be seen why establishment of methodologies is such an important element of the Software Quality Program.

Fortunately, many companies in the U.S. are beginning to recognize the importance of a establishing and implementing a defined process. Contrast the data of Reference 9 with the data first reported by the SEI in June, 1989 [11]. From that report, we see that 86% were found to be functioning at Level 1, and 13% at Level 2. At that time, fully 99% of the organizations surveyed did not have well-established, codified software development processes. This recent data shows a small but significant improvement in just a few years. Has this had a significant impact on quality, productivity, and cost? Very definitely! Consider the following examples: the Software Engineering Division of the Hughes Aircraft Ground Systems Group invested approximately $500,000 to move from Level 2 to Level 3 on the CMM. As a result of that investment, they have realized savings on the order of $2 million per year on their software development costs [12]. Raytheon's Equipment Division achieved a 7.7 return on investment in improving from Level 1 to Level 3, and realized a two-fold gain in productivity. With regard to the effect on quality, Raytheon eliminated approximately $15.8 million in rework costs from the time they embarked on their process improvement initiative in 1988 through the end of 1992 [13].

Several reports recently released show that other companies are experiencing similar benefits from software process improvement. A recent report from the SEI documents anecdotal data from 13 commercial organizations, defense contractors, and DoD installations that indicate benefits in a number of categories [19]. These include categories such as productivity gains, reduction in time to market, and reduced defects in the delivered software. Results from studies performed by Logos International and others indicate gains in cost and schedule performance [20].

In Chapters 2 and 3, we will continue the discussion of the CMM, software process assessments, and process improvement.

What does the accomplishment of this element of the SQP entail? Establishing methodologies refers to the process of defining the methodologies to apply to the development, operation, and maintenance efforts. Their implementation is facilitated by codifying them in the form of standard practices and procedures, and training personnel in their use. Implementation of the methodologies may be further facilitated by the acquisition of tools compatible with the methodologies and the standard practices and procedures. Enforcement is accomplished through the commitment of corporate management. Management must consistently expect and demand the application of the selected methodologies from project to project, and resist the temptation to abandon the established practices under conditions of schedule pressure. Some tools, such as automated process environments, can facilitate the enforcement of the methodologies and the associated standard practices and procedures.

Consistent use of the selected methodologies from project to project does not mean that they are never improved, updated, or modified. The acquisition, development, or use of different methodologies is not precluded. In fact, if a process is never updated or improved, it may be counterproductive. Nonetheless, before these changes are made, the evaluation of the efficacy of these changes must be performed. Their introduction must be carefully scheduled.

In this discussion of methodologies, when we refer to "development effort," it means the requirements definition, design, and test activities of the project and the documentation produced during these activities. Development procedures refer to those needed to define how to establish requirements and to design, code, test, and document the software: utilizing structured analysis, implementing top-down design, using software development folders [14], implementing coding standards, and configuration management.

"Operation" refers to production or operational usage of the software. Quality can be affected by improper operation of the software system or by inadequacies in instructions contained in the user's manual. Reference 3 illustrates this point quite well. It describes a situation where a large number of abnormal terminations occurred because the software was not correctly operated. In analyzing the cause of the errors, 78% of the errors could be classified as human error on the part of the operator or the user. These occurred because of an excessive number of manual steps in setting up the run or in processing it, making these operations cumbersome. Manual steps are, by nature, error prone. In this case, the inferior operability of the software adversely impacted the perception of its quality.

Reference 1 points out that if the software doesn't operate the way that the user of the system *expects*, it will *not* be perceived as quality software. As the example in Reference 3 showed, this can occur even if the software has been properly designed and coded, i.e., in compliance with the requirements. Operation of the software, therefore, is also a process that needs to be evaluated and improved, as necessary.

The maintenance activities pertain to those activities that occur after development has been completed and a production or operational baseline (or freeze) has been established for the software (code, design, documentation). At this point, acceptance or qualification testing has been completed and the software is ready for operational or production usage. If adequate procedures have not been established to handle software maintenance, the quality initially built into the software product may suffer degradation. For example, inadequate change control procedures or inadequate definition of procedures to "fix" the code in the event of a failure, would result in such degradation.

One way in which the accomplishment of this element of the SQP can be facilitated is by establishing a Software Engineering Process Group* (SEPG) [4]. It is the focal point for the methodology element of the SQP. Its main function is to serve as the initiator, sustainer, and evaluator of process change. Based on data collected through the means described by the software quality evaluation element of the SQP, the SEPG determines if the established processes for software development and maintenance are satisfying the quality requirements, especially in the form of product quality. If they are not, the SEPG researches other viable methodologies to determine a suitable replacement. It also evaluates new methodologies as they become available to determine their applicability to the company's products, and their capability to meet quality criteria. If the introduction of a new methodology can effect a material improve-

---

* In MIS organizations, it may be known as the MIS Standards Committee. It may be known by other names, as well, in other organizations, but its functions are essentially the same, no matter what it is called. For ease of reference, it will be referred to as the SEPG.

ment in product quality, the SEPG may recommend its introduction. In making this recommendation, it examines the impact of introducing the new methodology to determine if that will create excessive disruption, and significantly degrade the accomplishment of ongoing projects.

The methodologies, which are established by the SEPG, are established for use throughout the entire organization, but may be different for the various types of software produced by the organization. In other words, "one size fits all" doesn't necessarily apply when it comes to software process. The SEPG may identify the need for application domain-specific methodologies. For example, a company which produces software that controls nuclear reactors may utilize different methodologies for developing the software used in reactors from those used to develop their business-related information systems. Furthermore, it may be necessary, at the outset of a new project, to modify these methodologies to suit the unique requirements of the software to be produced on this new project. This is referred to as tailoring. Depending on the criticality and complexity of the software, practices may be added to or deleted from the defined "standard" process. Such decisions, however, require the review and approval of a centralized authority.

Considering the present state of the art, selecting appropriate methodologies to apply is, at best, a crude art, particularly for organizations at the lower levels of the CMM. It is based on experience, intuition, literature search, and common knowledge. No formalized techniques exist for specifying the methodologies to apply.

1.2.3 Evaluation of Process and Product Quality

The third element pertains to those activities necessary to evaluate the software development process and the resultant products. This element is referred to as the software quality evaluation (SQE) program. SQE is a set of assessment and measurement activities performed throughout software development and maintenance to evaluate the quality of software products and to evaluate associated documentation, processes, and activities that impact the quality of the products. "Assessment" pertains to qualitative evaluation while "measurement" pertains to quantitative evaluation.

Measurement encompasses all quantitative evaluations, specifically, tests, demonstrations, metrics, and inspections. For these kinds of activities, direct measures can be recorded and compared against pre-established values to determine if the software meets the requirements. Accordingly, unit level testing, software integration, and software performance testing can be considered as measurement activities. Similarly, the output of a compare program or a path analyzer program can also be considered measurement.

Measurement also includes the use of metrics and measures that can be used to directly determine the attainment of numerical software quality goals. Measures of reliability, such as the number of faults per 1000 lines of source code (faults/KSLOC), are examples of such measures. Chapters 4, 5, and 6 discuss the use of such measures.

On the other hand, any evaluative undertaking that requires reasoning or subjective judgment to reach a conclusion as to whether the software meets requirements is considered to be an assessment. It includes analyses, audits, surveys, and both document and project reviews.

The "set of evaluation activities" refers to the actions, such as reviews, evaluation, test, analysis, inspections, and so on, which are performed to determine that (1) technical requirements have been established, (2) products and processes conform to these established technical requirements, and ultimately, (3) to determine software quality. The focus of these activities vary as a function of the stage of the development effort. For instance, peer reviews conducted during the software requirements analysis activities will focus on the adequacy of the evolving software processing requirements and their compatibility with the requirements for the design of the database(s). On the other hand, peer reviews conducted during detailed design will focus on how well the design of each unit of software is implementing the requirements allocated to it.

These evaluations may be performed by a number of different organizations or functions, some or all of which may be within the project organization. Furthermore, any one evaluation may be performed by different organizations or functions. As an example, the evaluators of a software requirements specification for a flight control system may include a flight controls engineer (to ensure that all the technical requirements have been implemented), a software engineer (to ensure that the requirements, as specified, can be implemented in software), a test engineer (to ensure testability), and SQA (to ensure that the overall requirements for the content of the document, as well as it's quality, have been addressed). The "set of evaluation activities" to be performed are generally documented in project plans, software development plans, project-specific software quality procedures, and/or company quality plans and related software quality procedures.

In the case of the products, determination of the software quality can be performed by comparing the products against pre-established criteria. However, evaluation of product quality is difficult, especially since the definition of software quality is hard to express quantitatively within the current state-of-the-art. A large volume of research has been directed toward the establishment of quantitative definitions of quality, for example, software reliability. We see much of this effort expressed in terms of software metrics. Numerous definitions for software metrics have been proposed and applied to specific cases. No one set of metrics will work for all cases. There is no silver bullet that will satisfy everyone's needs. (In later chapters of this book, we will discuss some of these metrics and measures, and illustrate how they can be applied).

On the other hand, the technology is available to establish and enforce various forms of meaningful quality criteria. The approach is relatively straight forward: Establish criteria based upon measurable entities; entities that lend themselves to validation during software development. As long as these criteria can be related to the attribute of quality desired ("quality is in the eye of the beholder"), a project can use them to gauge quality. For example, the cyclomatic complexity metric is a measurable entity. Experience indicates that a limit of seven for cyclomatic complexity is wise to impose for units and aggregates of avionics software. At levels above seven, the software is more error-prone and more difficult to maintain. Accordingly, avionics software development projects would likely use this limit of the metric as one measure of the software product's quality.

The evaluation program also includes assessment and measurement of the software development and maintenance processes and the activities/procedures comprising them. It may be that the process is being properly implemented, but the products are not attaining the desired level of quality. These evaluations constitute a check of the existing process against the initial analysis performed prior to the start of the development, that is, during the methodology selection process discussed above. A principle of quality management is that product quality can be improved through the continuous improvement of the processes used to produce it. Continuous improvement is achieved by focusing on the processes, and using product evaluations, as necessary, as indicators of process adequacy. This evaluation may be implemented by examining interim software products, such as initial specifications, materials presented at walkthroughs or inspections, or the artifacts (products) which result from the process itself, such as software development folders. Such measurements are aimed at determining the quality of the content of these products as the determinant of the process quality.

Generally, the basis for determining which process to implement has been to look at a candidate process or set of processes and evaluate the proposed process on the basis of its track record. The assumption is that if the process has been shown to produce "high quality software" in the past, then proper implementation of the process will result in a high quality product. This argument is somewhat misleading. There has been anecdotal evidence [20] of the relationship, but no conclusive demonstration of a definite link between the process selected for the software development and the resultant quality of the software product itself. Establishment of such links has been more heuristic or intuitive rather than analytical. For example, the use of the Ada programming language promotes information hiding which, in turn, should make the software more adaptable. But, the actual cause and effect link has not been clearly demonstrated through hypothesis testing.

Typical of the difficulty in such research is the work of the Department of Defense (specifically the Air Force) in defining a software quality framework leading to software quality metrics (see for example, Reference 16). Upon close examination, it may be seen that this framework actually measures the adherence to good programming practices rather than the actual quality of the software. Other work attempting to link processes to product quality can be found in Reference 15.

What is crucial to any software development project is the definition and implementation of the activities necessary to assess and measure the quality of the software products produced by that project, in accordance with the requirements established for the project. Equally crucial is the definition and implementation of the activities necessary to evaluate the adequacy of the processes used by that project to produce the software products.

1.3 SUMMARY

In implementing the Software Quality Program, certain concepts must be kept in mind.

First, one must understand what software quality is and the technical aspects of specifying, designing, and testing for it. Software quality is achieved with proper software design and implementing appropriate processes. Quality cannot be achieved by "assuring" and testing the product. The relationship of product quality to process is indispensable.

Second, the ideas associated with software quality lead to the software quality program. General principles of such a program have been discussed. Three elements of the Software Quality Program were described in some detail; these elements interact not only with each other but also with all other project activities. This interaction is extremely complex, occurring at many levels within the software project and throughout the project's life. What one derives from the fact of this interaction is that no process is performed in a vacuum, nor is it an island unto itself. If we decompose the overall process into constituent sub-processes and activities, we will see that there are many suppliers to and customers of the development and maintenance activities performed during a software product's life cycle.

In this first chapter, we have set the stage for the remainder of the book. The SQP describes the framework for building quality software and determining the degree to which that "quality" has been obtained. The interdependence of this framework with process is very clear.

We will now turn our attention to describing what software processes consist of, and the ways by which these processes can be evaluated and improved.

REFERENCES

1. Baker, Emanuel R. and Fisher, Matthew J. "A Software Quality Framework," in *Concepts-The Journal of Defense Systems Acquisition Management*, Moore, Robert Wayne, ed.; Vol. 5, No. 4, Autumn, 1982 (Fort Belvoir VA: Defense Systems Management College, 1982).
2. Bryan, William E., and Siegel, Stanley G. "Software Configuration

Management—A Practical Look," in *The Handbook of Software Quality Assurance*, Schulmeyer, G. Gordon and McManus, James I., eds., New York: Van Nostrand Reinhold Company, Inc., 2nd ed., 1992.

3. McCabe, Thomas J., and Schulmeyer, G. Gordon. "The Pareto Principle Applied to Software Quality Assurance," in *The Handbook of Software Quality Assurance*, Schulmeyer, G. Gordon and McManus, James I., eds., New York: Van Nostrand Reinhold Company, Inc., 2nd ed., 1992.

4. Humphrey, Watts S. "Managing the Software Process," New York; Addison-Wesley, 1989.

5. Paulk, Mark C., Curtis, Bill, Chrissis, Mary Beth, and Weber, Charles V. "Capability Maturity Model for Software, Version 1.1," Technical Report CMU/SEI-93-TR-24. Software Engineering Institute, Carnegie Mellon University, February 1993.

6. Paulk, Mark C., Weber, Charles V., Garcia, Suzanne M., Chrissis, Mary Beth, and Bush, Marilyn. "Key Practices of the Capability Maturity Model, Version 1.1," Technical Report CMU/SEI-93-TR-25. Software Engineering Institute, Carnegie Mellon University, February 1993.

7. Humphrey, W. S.. and W. L. Sweet. "A Method for Assessing the Software Engineering Capability of Contractors," Technical Report CMU/SEI-87-TR-23. Software Engineering Institute, Carnegie Mellon University, September 1987.

8. Humphrey, Watts S. and David H. Kitson. "Preliminary Report on Conducting SEI-Assisted Assessments of Software Engineering Capability," Technical Report CMU-SEI-87-TR-16. Software Engineering Institute, Carnegie Mellon University, July 1987.

9. "Process Maturity Profile of the Software Community 1997 Update," Software Engineering Measurement and Analysis Team, Software Engineering Institute, Carnegie Mellon University, October 1997.

10. Yacobellis, Robert E. "A White Paper on U.S. vs. Japan Software Engineering," January 1990.

11. Tutorial. "Software Process Assessment," Software Engineering Institute, Carnegie Mellon University, September 1990.

12. Humphrey, Watts S., Snyder, Terry R., and Willis, Ron R. "Software Process Improvement at Hughes Aircraft," *IEEE Software*, Vol. 8, No. 4, July, 1991.

13. Dion, Raymond. "Process Improvement and the Corporate Balance Sheet," *IEEE Software*, Vol. 10, No. 4, July, 1993.

14. Ingrassia, Frank S., The Unit Development Folder (UDF); "An Effective Management Tool for Software Development," in *Tutorial; Software Management*, Reifer, Donald J. ed., 3rd ed., Washington, DC; IEEE Computer Society Press, 1986.

15. Arthur, James D. and Richard E. Nance. "Developing an Automated Procedure for Evaluating Software Development Methodologies and Associated Products," Technical Report SRC-87-007. System Research Center, Virginia Polytechnic Institute, Blacksburg, VA, 16 April 1987.

16. Bowen, Thomas P., Wigle, Gary B., and Tsai, Jay T. "Specification of Software Quality Attributes," Technical Report RADC-TR-85-37, Rome Air Development Center, Griffis Air Force Base, Rome, NY, February 1985.

17. Humphrey, Watts S. "A Software Process Maturity Model," *IEEE Software*, Vol. 10, No. 4, July, 1987.

18. Sims, D., "Motorola India Self-Assesses at Level 5," *IEEE Software*, March, 1994, Page 92.

19. Herbsleb, James, et al., "Benefits of CMM-Based SPI: Initial Results," SEI 94-TR-13, 1994.

20. Zubrow, David, "Software Process Improvement: Business Impacts and Values," Software Engineering Institute, Presentation to the Los Angeles Software Process Improvement Network (SPIN), 29 May 1996.

2
Basics of Quality Management and Continuous Process Improvement

2.1 INTRODUCTION TO QUALITY MANAGEMENT CONCEPTS AND PRINCIPLES

2.1.1 Definitions of Quality

To begin the discussion of this section, let us review a basic concept from Chapter 1: The Definition of Software Quality.

There was an episode in the long-running hit television series, *M*∗*A*∗*S*∗*H*∗, in which Radar, the telepathic company clerk (an enlisted man), had a short-lived romance with a nurse (an officer). Radar, whose insecurities were best characterized by the teddy bear that he slept with every night, was feeling very insecure in this relationship. He really felt out of his league. She was an officer, and he wasn't. She was very sophisticated, and he wasn't. He wasn't sure that he could maintain a conversation with her, being that she was a college graduate, and his formal education fell far short of that. He knew very little of art or fine music, things that she was far more familiar with than was Radar, and he was worried that she would rapidly find him boring. Radar turns to Captain Hawkeye Pierce, M.D., for advice. Hawkeye, womanizer, prankster, and schemer extraordinaire, advises Radar to bluff his way through conversations with her, and make a direct move to a little romance. Hawkeye's rationale was that once she was hooked romantically, Radar's lack of sophistication and education would be unimportant. But Radar is uncertain. What if the conversation turns to classical music? Hawkeye advises him only to say, "Ahhhh! Bach!," in a very knowing tone.

"Ahhhh! Bach!" is, perhaps, the best way to describe quality. It's very difficult to define, but everyone will say that they know it when they see it, or hear it, or feel it. And often its very subjective. Ask people about quality who are satisfied with their cars, and they are likely to tell you about the looks of the car, or its ruggedness, or how fast it can go. They won't all necessarily use the same yardstick as the indicator of quality. Quality means different things to different people. Quality is in the eye of the beholder.

When we are talking about software, who is the beholder? It is, of course, the person using the software—the person who has to interact with the software every time it is executed. That is the person who must be satisfied that the software does what he or she wanted when it was purchased. In the case of software developed solely for internal use within a company or other entity, the determinant of quality is whether or not the software performs as intended when the user asked the development organization to produce it. In many cases these needs evolve with time and accumulated experience, creating a continuous need for upgrading and tailoring.

Typically, the user's perception of quality is, "Does the software do what I wanted it to do?" If it doesn't, the perception is that the software is not quality software. It is this concept that underlies the definition of software quality that appears in the first chapter: the degree to which a software product possesses a specified set of attributes necessary to fulfill a stated purpose. The "stated purpose" is, of course, the intended function of the software. Software product quality means, in effect, achieving its intended end use, as defined by the user or customer. These requirements include the software functional and performance requirements, and also include requirements for maintainability, portability, interoperability, and so on. The significance of this concept is that product requirements are, in reality, the quality requirements. And they must *accurately* capture and reflect the way that the user/customer wants to use the software.

The concepts underlying this definition of quality for software are very consistent with other definitions of software quality [1]. Virtually all of them address fitness of use for the customer or user in one way, shape, or form.

The ability (or inability) to accurately capture what the user or customer wants is one of the major process problems in software affecting quality. Various studies indicate that requirements-related errors account for anywhere from 25% to 40% of all defects found in software. Data collected by Capers Jones shows that requirements errors account for 30% of defects in MIS applications, 15% in systems software, 25% in military software, and 25% overall [2]. A study by Ray Rubey showed that incomplete or erroneous specification of requirements accounted for 28% of the defects observed on one project, and another 12% were due to intentional deviation from the specification [3]. Clearly, the data indicates that the real measure of software quality, i.e., accurately specifying what the user or customer wants, is not being met very well.

Consider the following complicating factors:

- As difficult as it is to capture the user's view of desired functionality in a single user system, it is significantly more difficult for a system with multiple users. *All* inputs (viewpoints) *must* be considered. Often, they are not.
- When software is being developed for commercial sale, the user community is a vast unknown population of people "out there." A go-between (and arbiter of what the users really want) is the company's sales and marketing organization. Unfortunately, they often have a fuzzy image of some grand and glorious product that will be ready in two months and will be incredibly cheaper than products offered by the competition. Another go-between is the product support organization—the people who staff the help lines. They spend their days listening to complaints. Often, the views of sales and marketing differ markedly from that of the product support organization, and the level of detail at which these views are presented also differ markedly. Identifying what the user community *really* wants, and to deliver precisely that on-schedule and within the budget allotted for the development effort, is to make order out of chaos.
- When software is developed under contract, the contract is an obstacle to defining the real quality measure—unless the requirements have been completely (and accurately) defined by the customer before the contract is let, or there is a mechanism for coming to agreement on the requirements with a minimum of contractual red tape.

- When software is developed under contract, sometimes the customer is not the user. This typically happens in defense contracts, where the organization or command responsible for acquiring the software is not the ultimate user of the software. Sometimes, the true needs get garbled in the translation from user to acquirer. Determining what the user *really* wants becomes a major headache.

Quality is in the eye of the beholder. Making sure the eventual "beholder" (the user) is able to obtain the quality that he or she expects is the challenge of software development. The real problem is being able to see the software product as the ultimate beholder or beholders will see it. And, often, being able to see it when they, the users, aren't able to articulate very well what they want to see.

2.1.2 Overview of Quality Management

Quality management can be traced back to Walter Shewhart who, while working at Bell Laboratories in the 20s, developed the concepts of process control and process improvement. Shewhart is credited as being the inventor of the control chart and the Plan-Do-Check-Act (PDCA) cycle. Edwards Deming and Joseph Juran taught the Japanese, in the 50s, how to implement these ideas of process control and process improvements. Deming's experience as a consultant in statistical methods is summarized in 14 management principles which are the basis of what is now called Total Quality Management. Juran developed many of the management tools and concepts of quality management which were published in the famous Juran Quality Control Handbook (see References 5, 12, and 14). Central to the implementation of quality management is the concept of a process with its "customers" and "suppliers." A process may be thought of as a set of activities organized to achieve some objective or goal. In manufacturing, it is the series of activities necessary to turn raw materials into objects which can be assembled for delivery to a customer. In software, it is the set of activities necessary to turn a concept into an executing application. The set of activities may be very rudimentary, or may be very complex. The maturity of the process and the kinds of activities included in the process can have an enormous bearing on the resultant quality of the product.

Establishing such structures of activities naturally creates an opportunity to establish feedback loops, both internal and external, around each process in an organization. These feedback loops help identify opportunities for improvements and provide information for controlling processes. Both the control and improvement of processes rely on the use of statistical methodology. The actual implementation of Statistical Process Control and successes in process improvement efforts demand a broad system view which requires an understanding of issues in human resources management, accounting procedures, and information systems. Speeding up the implementation of quality management is becoming a burning topic for many companies who are looking at quality breakthroughs as the way to improve their competitive position. Twenty years ago the ideas and tools of quality management were unknown or misunderstood in the West by both academics and industrialists. Nowadays, Deming and Juran are mentioned in most management textbooks, and Quality has become recognized as a major strategic dimension by modern enterprises who are forced to keep up with rapid changes and world competition.

2.1.3 The Quality Movement

Varying amounts of effort has been expended by organizations in process improvement, ranging from essentially nothing to full-blown, all out efforts. Information was gathered by the GAO [4] to provide the U.S. House of Representatives with a summary of the effectiveness of quality management in making American companies more competitive in domestic and world markets. The report is an overview of results of company adoption of quality management based on analyzing 59 small (500 or less employees) and large (500 or more employees) companies.

Some companies refused to divulge financial data. All companies reviewed had adopted quality management in the mid-1980s. The benefits of implementing quality management realized after 1–5 year "gestation" period are shown below in Table 2.1.

2.1.4 Organizing For Quality Management

In organizing for quality management, it is essential that the structure be organized to focus on the fundamental purpose of quality management: achieving continuous process improvement. Quality,

Table 2.1   Performance Indicators

Measure	Average change
A. Employee relations	
1. Employee satisfaction	1.4% increase
2. Attendance	0.1% increase
3. Employee turnover	0.6% decrease
4. Safety and health rates	1.8% increase
5. Suggestions	16.6% increase
B. Operating procedures	
1. Reliability	11.3% increase
2. On-time delivery	4.7% increase
3. Order-processing time	12.0% decrease
4. Errors or defects	10.3% decrease
5. Product lead time	5.8% decrease
6. Inventory turnover	7.2% increase
7. Cost of poor quality	9.0% decrease
C. Customer satisfaction	
1. Overall customer satisfaction	2.5% increase
2. Customer complaints	11.6% decrease
D. Financial performance	
1. Market share	13.7% increase
2. Sales per employee	8.6% increase
3. Return on asset	1.3% increase

as practiced by most software organizations, is focused on problem correction. Problem correction, while essential, only serves to remove the defects that have been embedded in the product as a consequence of the production and/or development process. Problem prevention, on the other hand, serves to improve the quality of the product and improve the competitive position of the organization. When properly organized for quality management, the focus of organizations is on problem prevention.

Problem prevention has two aspects: (1) Preventing *recurrence* of existing problems, and (2) preventing *introduction* of new problems. In other words, problem prevention results in quality improvement. Quality improvement can be considered to be of two types: *reactive* (driven by problems) and *proactive* (driven by the desire to improve quality). Reactive quality improvement is the process of understanding a specific quality defect, fixing the product, and identifying and eliminating the root cause to prevent recurrence. Proactive quality improvement is the continual cycle of identifying opportunities and implementing changes throughout the product realization process which result in fundamental improvements in the level of product quality. It is a continual process.

Quality improvement necessitates some organizational structural changes. The first is the implementation of a *Quality Council*. Other names used for such forums are Continuous Improvement Committee, Quality Board, and Quality Management Forum. Sometimes, the role of the Quality Council is split between management and the lower level performing organizations. In these cases, management may assume the role of a steering committee, whereas the performer level may be responsible for overseeing the details of the process improvement activities. Specifically, in software development and maintenance organizations, it is common to find Software Engineering Process Groups (SEPGs) or Software Engineering Committees which operate in this capacity of Quality Councils. The management steering committee may set process improvement goals, provide budgets and other resources, and be the final approval authority for the proposed process improvement projects, and the SEPG or Software Engineering Committee will act as the administrative arm of process improvement.

Overall, the Quality Council is responsible for:

- Defining and helping implement the improvement process
- Initiating improvements (some)
- Supporting the improvement process
- Keeping the process going and tracking progress
- Disseminating information
- Gathering data

Specifically, the Quality Council's charter is to:

- Establish a system for choosing projects, appointing project teams, and soliciting and screening nominations for projects.
- Set responsibilities for carrying out projects by defining team charters and appointing facilitators, team members, and team leaders.
- Identify training needs, plan the training, and identify the trainees.

- Establish support for project teams.
- Provide for coordination of process improvement efforts.
- Establish measures for progress on improvement.
- Design a plan for publicity and recognition of achievements.

To facilitate the accomplishment of these responsibilities, an additional organizational entity must exist: the Quality Improvement Teams (QIT). These are ad hoc teams that are commissioned by and are responsible to the Quality Council to implement specific process improvement projects. The QITs are responsible for:

- Initiating improvements
- Understanding the problems
- Determining causes and solutions
- Estimating the benefits for specific process improvements and securing support
- Addressing people issues
- Implementing the change
- Establishing methods to maintain the level of improvement
- Tracking progress

Organizational structures and entities in and of themselves are not sufficient. Other factors must exist in order to accomplish successful process improvement. Chief among these are the commitment and involvement of management. Without that, virtually nothing is possible. Lip service on the part of management will be readily recognized; consequently, there will be no motivation for the organization to implement any changes in the way they do business. "Talking the talk" without "walking the walk" will be recognized as empty words. Management must exhibit the following behavioral characteristics to ensure that the organization understands that they are sincerely committed to process improvement:

- Commitment must be genuine and self-evident.
- Guidance, support, and training through close involvement must be provided.
- Keep team focused on business objectives.
- Establish a relationship of trust and respect between all members.
- Acknowledge all recommendations.

2.2 THE IMPROVEMENT PROCESS

The improvement process can be characterized in a number of ways. Joseph M. Juran [5] describes process improvement in what he refers to as the "Quality Journey." The basic attributes of organizations on the Quality Journey can be described as follows.

1. They have a plan to keep improving all operations continuously. No company can afford to sit on their laurels and assume that they have to perform process improvement one time only. It's important to stay ahead of the competition.
2. A system for measuring these improvements accurately. It's important to be able to assess the return on investment.
3. A strategic plan based on benchmarks that compare the organization's performance with the world's best. To stay ahead of the competition, a company must have information on how well they are doing relative to their competition.
4. A close partnership with suppliers and customers, that feeds improvements back into operation. If a company improves the quality of their part of a product, but a supplier of an included component doesn't do the same, the quality of the total product will be degraded.
5. A deep understanding of the customers so that their wants can be translated into products and services. A good supplier is attuned to their marketplace and aware of the needs of it. Nobody will buy a product or service just for the sake of buying it. It at least has to successfully fill some identified need.
6. A long-lasting relationship with customers, going beyond the delivery of the product and service. A hotel, for example, may provide excellent service. But if the guest feels like he or she is just a room number, the guest may go elsewhere in the future.
7. A focus on preventing mistakes rather than merely correcting them. A supplier who makes constant mistakes, and cheerfully rectifies them quickly, will eventually lose out to the supplier who doesn't make the mistakes. The customer

resents having to take productive time out of the day to call the supplier because of their mistakes.
8. A commitment to improving quality that runs from top to bottom in the organization.

The improvement process itself transitions through several steps. They are as follows:

- Problem recognition
- Project selection
- Diagnosis
- Preparing the people
- Implementing the solution
- Maintaining the improvement

In this section, we will discuss these steps as they apply to process improvement in general. In a later section, we will discuss these steps in more detail as they apply to software process improvement, specifically.

2.2.1 Problem Recognition

Clearly, the course of process improvement must begin with the recognition of an existing problem or a potential problem. While process improvement in and of itself is highly desirable, organizations will not begin process improvement without some external motivator. The more enlightened organizations guard their market position, and the potential loss of that is generally sufficient motivation. For the less sophisticated organizations, process improvement doesn't begin until a problem of near-crisis proportions occurs.

There are some typical signs that are indicators of existing or potential problems. One is the recognition that production costs are higher than those of competitors for the same products. Another is an indication that competitors are gaining a larger share of the market. This can sometimes result from higher production costs, necessitating an increase in the price paid by customers. High warranty costs are another indication. When delivered products have to be returned to the manufacturer for rework during the warranty period at a relatively frequent rate, or the warranty period has to be shortened to reduce overhead, it's a sure indication that process improvement is in order. In the case of software, it could be unexpected field modifications or frequent updates to the delivered software to re-move "bugs."

The foregoing would suggest that tracking the cost of quality is in order. Rough numbers can often be more than adequate. Simply put, the cost of quality is the comparison of the costs of preventing problems from occurring against the cost of defect removal. Clearly, when the cost of defect removal exceeds the cost of defect prevention by a good margin, the cost of quality is too high. Too much effort is being put into correcting errors and not enough into preventing them. This is exacerbated by the fact that the cost of correction increases exponentially the later in the life cycle that the problem is detected.

When we talk of defect prevention, we are talking of activities such as the cost of establishing a defined software development process along with the attendant cost of evaluating the quality of the products during development and when they are ready for delivery. Included in that would be the cost of testing, as an example. The cost of defect removal includes activities such as rework, updating documentation, and retest.

The objective of tracking the cost of quality is to reduce the necessity for and the cost of rework. Obviously, a related objective is the reduction of the costs for quality evaluation. When good software development practices are followed during requirements analysis and design, for example, the amount of effort expended in testing is reduced.

For a more detailed discussion of cost of quality models as applied to software, see Reference 6.

In addition to tracking the cost of quality, other types of information can provide valuable insight into existing and potential problems. These would include:

- Field reports
- Inspection and audit results
- Data on manufacturing yields
- Information on new technology
- Data on competitors' products
- Customer satisfaction reports

Field reports provide information on problems users are experiencing with the product, while inspection and audit reports provide information that can indicate process problems. Data on manufacturing yields can provide insight into potential rework problems during the manufacturing process. In the case of software, this would apply to the process of replicating the production-status software. Information on new technology could indicate areas where technology solutions can facilitate the process improvement effort. Data on competitors' products would indicate areas where the competition might be achieving an edge over the organization. Finally, customer satisfaction reports provide information on customer happiness with the product, as well as potential new features that the customers might like to see in the product.

The data from these sources should be analyzed and existing and potential problem areas identified. Identified problem areas should be documented. As indicated earlier, the costs of poor quality should be estimated.

For software, another source exists for the identification of existing and potential problems. This is the use of the CBA-IPI, an overview of which was presented in Chapter 1. This will be discussed in greater detail later in Chapter 3, together with a description of how this assessment process can be utilized to initiate process improvement projects, utilizing many of the principles discussed in this chapter.

2.2.2   Selection of an Improvement Project

In this section, we present some general principles with respect to selection of improvement projects. In the next chapter, we present this concept in more detail.

The selection of an improvement project begins with an informal analysis or a structured assessment, which determines the current status of the state of practice within the organization. The results of the analysis, or assessment, are a set of findings, which characterize the strengths and weaknesses of the processes currently operating in the organization. The weaknesses suggest the need for improvement. As a consequence, there is usually a need to nominate improvement projects. The action planning which results from the assessment establishes priorities for process improvement and for the selection of improvement projects. Those which are initiated first should be those which are likely to have a high return on investment (ROI). Various analytical methods can be used in conjunction with the planning process. These methods can include, for example, Pareto analyses, Process Mappings, Impact Analysis, etc. Pareto analyses may be based on potential reduction in Cost of Quality (COQ) or simple ROI. Other factors which enter into the picture with regard to prioritization may include ease of implementation or urgency to implement a change (e.g., sudden drop in quality, increased cost of production or customer mandated requests.).

Having selected and prioritized a set of improvement projects, it is then necessary to secure management approval. This involves preparing project descriptions and providing cost/benefit estimates for each proposed project. A quality improvement team should be identified for each proposed project, as well. To ensure that the quality improvement effort will succeed, it is necessary to obtain the commitment of management to provide the needed resources, including the commitment of time for the personnel having the required skills and capabilities to implement the project. Accordingly, the project descriptions will identify members and assignments for the implementation team.

2.2.3 Structured Diagnosis

Performing a CBA-IPI will result in the identification of specific problem areas, their symptoms, and their consequences (past, present, and potential). This structured assessment will point the improvement effort in the direction of specific process areas that need improvement, such as the type of project management functions that should be included in project planning. The CBA-IPI assessment relies on the collection of data and analysis of symptoms. This comes about through the analysis of current and historical data. Often, during the period when the improvement project is being planned in detail, or even in the early stages of the plan's implementation, new data may have to be created. This facilitates focusing in on the root causes of the process problems observed. Measurement data helps quantify the extent of the problems and their effects. Such measurements should be made with greater precision than may have been utilized for data collected previously. Parameters not normally considered may have to be measured. Abnormal conditions and their effects may also have to be considered, and included as part of the measurements made.

Once the process improvement project begins, the existing process to be improved needs to be studied in detail. This may include developing models of the process and forming theories about the causes of the problems observed. Theory development may utilize techniques such as brainstorming, cause and effect diagrams, and force field analyses. The most promising theories should then be selected and tested. This can be accomplished utilizing Pareto analyses, conducting experiments, and collecting and analyzing new data.

The intent is identify the root causes of the process problems and propose solutions. When the process improvement projects were identified, first cut solutions for the problems were proposed. This effort results in a refinement of the proposed solution—one that is based on detailed data.

2.2.4 Preparing People—Guidelines for Introducing Change

Implementing change is not done easily. People in an organization may often talk about the need for change, but often, the changes they would like to see are changes that "other people need to make." In order to implement change effectively, it is essential to be cognizant of the people aspect—cognizant of the fact that changes are likely to cause disruption: disruption in how people perceive things, and how they behave (Figure 2.1).

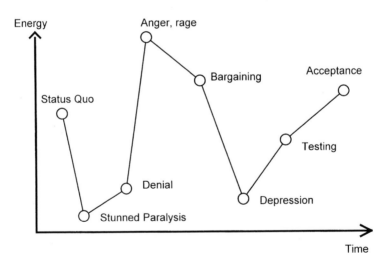

Figure 2.1   Reaction to change from initial exposure to acceptance.

There are a number of things to be cognizant of regarding the behavior of people when it comes to change introduction. The following list addresses most of these concerns:

1. Be aware of the existence of a culture in the affected organization. The existing culture will greatly influence the ability to introduce change. A culture that values the "cowboy" approach to software development will resist efforts to introduce structure and discipline into the development process. Be aware that a change which affects the pattern of behavior of a culture will generate resistance.

2. Be aware that the real causes of resistance are frequently not stated. For instance, strong resistance to the introduction of peer reviews may reflect a fear on the part of those resisting that an objectively conducted review may expose them. They may not be the competent developers they have made themselves out to be. Consequently, it is important to identify which aspects of the culture will be threatened. Proposed changes should specifically address the benefits which offset these threats.

3. Secure active participation of members of the culture during planning and implementation. Establish an environment where people at all levels can feel that they had a share in the activity. Everyone then becomes an owner of the process improvement effort.

4. Start with a small implementation, for example, a pilot project. Use results to secure wider acceptance.

5. Use specific techniques to gain acceptance of the process improvement effort. Remedy specific causes of resistance. Utilize persuasion when necessary. Offer additional desirable changes. Provide an environment where the culture can be changed (e.g., by education or by showing how life will be made easier as a result).

6. Allow time to achieve acceptance. Don't expect overnight results.

7. Avoid surprises. Surprises can often be an effective way of creating obstacles to achieving the desired goals. Don't spring changes on the organization without warning.

8. Energy levels vary over time as organizations move to achieve acceptance after a challenge to the status quo has

been initiated. A striking analogy to how organizations re-act to change can be derived from a model developed by Kubler-Ross [7], which describes how people with fatal ill-nesses prepare themselves for death. The model is pictured in Figure 2.1. Many organizations will recognize specific examples of how they faced the challenge: going through the stages of denial, anger, bargaining, depression, and fi-nally acceptance of the much needed change.

2.2.5 Process Improvement Projects

Process improvement projects are structured to address specific problem areas. For instance, if the requirements definition activity results in poorly defined requirements, designs and subsequent im-plementations in code will be in error. Process improvement in this case would focus on improving the ability to define requirements more accurately.

In order to accomplish improvements, measures of the existing process and changes to it must exist. This requires that we:

1. Study the current process and its outputs to identify vari-ables related to quality
2. Develop measures of those variables
3. Create a format to collect data

Processes have either "common cause variation" or "special cause variation." Common causes are in the system itself. Examples of common causes include the consistency of applying standards to the development process, or the training given to the developers. Special causes refer to variables that are not part of the system. Examples of special causes include the required use of customer-furnished software which turns out to have poor quality, a malfunc-tioning workstation, or a new developer using inappropriate proce-dures.

Typically, actions on special causes can be dealt with at the worker or first supervisory level. Actions on common causes usually involve major changes that require the attention of higher manage-ment. Special causes are dealt with first so that the process can be stabilized. It is then possible to address common causes and improve overall performance.

After the process changes, management must evaluate the effect of the change relative to the original goals. If the changes lead to improvements, then steps are taken to make the changes permanent. We standardize the changes. If there has been no significant improvement, then other possible causes must be investigated. Changes could include changing standards, work methods, suppliers, or providing new training to developers.

Once a process has been improved, the improvement must be maintained. We monitor the process to make sure we hold the gains we have made. Data collection for monitoring is expected to be a regular task of the people involved in implementing the process.

Process improvement efforts are a continuous activity for everyone. Employees at all level should be continuously searching for new ideas, improvement opportunities, and identification of customer needs.

2.2.6 Maintaining the Level of Improvement

Behavioral psychology studies how learning is accomplished. It often does this by studying animal behavior in controlled settings and extending their findings to human life. One form of learning is referred to as operant conditioning. In operant conditioning, a reward is given for performing a desired act. For instance, laboratory rats may be trained to press a lever in order to receive a food pellet. Pressing the lever is the desired behavior, and the receipt of the food pellet is the reward. Training, in this instance, will begin with the rat receiving a food pellet for every lever press. It will then progress to where the rat receives a pellet for every X number of presses, and then proceed to where the rat is receiving reinforcement for the desired behavior on a random schedule.

It has often been observed that when rats progress to the point where they are on a random reinforcement schedule, the rat will effectively rest for a short period of time after getting the reward before beginning the lever pressing again. This is generally not a function of the rat's hunger level, but more of a basking in the glow of having achieved something.

There are parallels here for process improvement. Many organizations achieve some initial level of process improvement, and then rest on their laurels. Far too often, the resting period becomes so long that process improvement is eventually abandoned. It is not enough just to achieve an initial level of improvement—it must be sustained.

There are a number of ways of maintaining the energy level. One way is to measure performance regularly. As improvements occur, and figures become available to show how much improvement has occurred, this often helps to serve as reinforcement for the effort. Consequently, it is also important to publicize quality improvement success. Without the feedback, the effort can soon die on the vine. People will begin to feel that nothing has occurred or that the improvement was implemented, but not successfully.

Use new standards of performance. Compare current activity with new standards. For instance, if the old standard of performance was to produce code that went into beta test with a fault density of 6 defects per thousand lines of code, and after one year of process improvement, the quality had improved to 4.5 defects per thousand lines of code, the new level should become the standard. It becomes a real challenge to better the improved levels of performance.

Correct problems quickly to maintain performance. There are two reasons for this. One is to recognize achievement. As was pointed out in the previous paragraph, if the organization is producing at higher levels of quality, it is essential to maintain that level. Providing encouragement for good performance is fundamental. By the same token, when problems arise that adversely affect new, improved levels of performance, that must be corrected as soon as possible. Allowing problems to fester will only demotivate.

The second reason is to help other parts of the organization with similar problems. Utilization of "lessons learned" is an important part of infusing process improvement throughout the entire organization.

Reinforcement of process improvement involves periodic reassessment. In other words, start the process improvement cycle again. Quality improvement must become a continual cycle. Assess the present situation. Determine the degree to which process improvement has been achieved. Don't look only for problems, but look also for situations in which potential problems can be prevented. Look for the proactive improvement opportunities, as well as reactive improvements. Review the priorities of the remaining improvement project proposals in light of the new data. Perhaps some of the

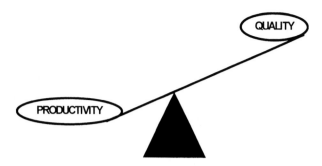

Figure 2.2 What many believe.

priorities will have changed. Perhaps some new process improvement project having a higher priority will be required.

2.2.7 Quality Gets Results

There is a mistaken notion to the effect that if orderly processes are introduced into the daily work environment, quality may go up, but productivity will go down. The flip side of this notion is that if productivity goes up, quality will decrease. These notions are illustrated in Figures 2.2 and 2.3. In actuality, neither are true. Improvement in quality results in improvement in productivity (see Figure 2.4).

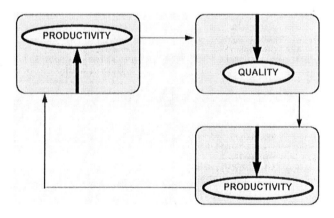

Figure 2.3 The apparent dilemma.

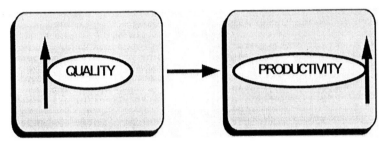

Figure 2.4   Resolving the quality–productivity dilemma.

There are many examples that can be utilized to describe the benefits experienced by hardware manufacturing companies, service organizations, and software houses. We will focus on examples from the software industry. The following are some examples of the benefits that have accrued to these software organizations from process improvement, i.e., improvement in quality *and* productivity.

- Hughes Aircraft Co., in Fullerton, CA, invested $500,000 in software process improvement and reduced project overruns by $2 million/year.
- Raytheon Equipment Division, Software Systems Laboratory, invested $1.1 million in software process improvement and reduced the 1990 cost of non-conformance by $8.2 million, resulting in a return on investment (ROI) of 7.7.
- Fujitsu: In the late seventies, 40% of software projects were over budget and behind schedule. Five years later they reduced it to 15%, and slashed defect rates by a factor of 10 (through the use of increased code and design reviews).
- IBM Federal Systems Division produced 500,000 lines of source code (500 KSLOC) for use in the on-board space shuttle systems, and 1.7 million lines of source code (MSLOC) for ground support systems. Through a focus on early detection (over 85% of errors are discovered prior to integration build), they reduced defects from 2/KSLOC to 0.11/KSLOC in three years.
- AT&T Network Software Center: Implemented over 100 quality improvement projects in the late 1980's. As a consequence, they succeeded in reducing open faults from 700 in 1989 to 200 in 1991, and reduced the development cycle from two years to 6 months.

Conversely, we find that the failure to improve quality is costly. The 1979 GAO report [8] found that in a sample of $6.77 million worth of information systems software projects for the Department of Defense (DoD), only 2% of the projects were ultimately delivered in usable condition. Almost a third were paid for but never delivered. Almost 50% were delivered but never used, because the amount of rework required to make them useful was prohibitive. A more recent study [9] found that the situation had not changed very much since the earlier study had been performed. It was findings such as these that contributed to initiating the projects sponsored by the DoD to foster process improvement. One such project resulted in the establishment of the Capability Maturity Model (CMM) and associated assessment methodologies.

T. Capers Jones [10,18], reports that canceled projects consume 15% of all software efforts in the US each year, costing some $14.3 billion and a loss of 285,000 person years in programming time. In general, the larger the project, the greater is the probability of cancellation. For small systems, the cancellation rate is around 7%. For large systems in excess of one million source lines of code, the cancellation rate approached 50%, and 65% for even larger systems. These included operating systems, telecommunications systems, major defense systems, and the like. Projects are canceled for a variety of reasons, such as the need for the application disappearing. But many of the causes relate to poor process implementation, such as enormous cost overruns, or the application being too far behind schedule.

Clearly, there is a significant cost to organizations for failure to implement process improvement—or even to take a first look at how well their processes are working for them.

2.2.8 Senior Management Involvement

Institutionalizing process improvement requires the proactive involvement of senior management. Everyone has heard the age-old adage that quality is everybody's business. It is not the sole function of the Quality Assurance organization or the software developers or senior management. *Everyone* must be involved.

It is especially important that senior management be involved. Management must lead the way. Management's actions indicate to the organization what their level of commitment is to the process improvement effort. The rest of the organization takes their cue from senior management. If senior management regards adherence to process as dispensable, no one in the organization will pay much attention to it. On the other hand, if senior management exhibits a strong commitment to process, the rest of the organization will follow. Management must also commit the necessary resources (funds, personnel, computer resources). Their support must be visible. The commitment to process and process improvement must be conveyed to lower levels of management. Their buy-in is essential for commitment to process to work. Middle management has often been called the "black hole" of management. If they don't buy in, or sense that management's commitment is not real, senior management's message will progress no lower.

It is not uncommon to see organizations where the senior manager has emphatically stated his or her commitment to process improvement, only to later pull the rug out from under the effort. For example, personnel who were assigned to process improvement projects are effectively told that they would have to do these activities in their spare time. Process improvement cannot be performed as a spare time activity. It must be done as a specific work assignment within the context of the normal work day. We have also seen senior managers state their commitment to process improvement, only to have their middle managers undercut the effort by stonewalling. The senior manager cannot merely state a dictum and not be actively involved. He or she must follow up with their lower level managers to ensure that they are implementing his or her requirements.

There is another aspect to proactive involvement: participation in the selection and implementation of the process improvement projects. We have alluded to this in Section 2.1.4. We will discuss more about that in the next chapter.

2.3 PROCESS MANAGEMENT

2.3.1 Overview of Process Management

A process is the organization of people, materials, machines and methods into work activities needed to produce a specific end result in a particular environment. When applied to software, it translates into "the total set of software engineering activities needed to transform a user's requirements into software" [11]. It is a repeated sequence of activities characterized as having measurable inputs, value added activities, and measurable outputs. Analyzing the process is the key to improvements.

Quick fixes to problems are how we have operated in the past, but quick fixes don't usually result in improving the process in the long-run and can actually result in a different problem surfacing elsewhere.

Analyzing the existing process is the first step and is the most important one. Flowcharting (or any other graphical process description) is generally an effective technique for analyzing the process. Flowcharting can identify duplication of work, steps that can be eliminated, and steps that may need to be standardized among branches, sections, etc. Analysis also should include identification of our customers and what they need and expect from us.

Knowledge of who the customers are and what their needs are is essential. It is very obvious that someone who comes into a store and buys an item is a customer, or that a company buying a "shrink-wrapped" accounting software package is a customer. But these are not the only types of people who are customers. Everyone is a customer and everyone is a supplier. For example, a software designer who performs design based on a system analyst's definition of the requirements is a customer. The customer is the designer and the system analyst is a supplier to the design group who will implement the requirements in design.

We can begin thinking of the next person in the process as a customer by asking ourselves the following questions:

- How does a change in what we do affect other parts of the process?
- Do we know what our rework rate is? (In terms of software, this relates for example to correction of defects in the design or the code).
- What is causing the problems?

Analyzing the process provides answers. In performing this analysis, we have to learn how to deal with facts, not assumptions. Part of the way of doing this is to rely on feedback related to the process, that is, feedback from the customers and suppliers that participate in the process. To measure progress, we need to know what, how, and when to measure. We need facts or data to know how the system is operating, and why. Do we know how our customers expect us to perform and how well we are meeting their expectations?

Addressing these questions aids in the development of a quality improvement plan. A well-developed plan enables an organization to concentrate its resources on achieving quality improvements by establishing measurable goals. The following are examples of measurable goals:

- Reducing elapsed time for different activities in the software development process
- Shortening delivery time
- Reducing error rates

Goals must be measurable and relevant to your mission. They should provide a direct benefit to the customer. The achievement of quality goals will require changes in process performance. A critical task of management is to identify and define these needed changes.

2.3.2 Strategic Quality Planning

This section discusses the strategic planning process for software quality improvement. The emphasis is on quality improvements. The processes of quality planning and quality control are only briefly referenced. Quality improvement is the organized creation of beneficial changes in process performance levels. Quality planning, on the other hand, is the activity of determining customer needs and the development of products and processes required to meet those needs. Finally, quality control is defined as the managerial process during which actual process performance is evaluated and actions are taken on unusual performance. (For more details on topics of quality management see Juran [12]).

Godfrey [13] lists seven milestones that delineate a road map for the top management of organizations planning their journey towards quality improvement. With some modifications, these milestones are:

- *Awareness* of the competitive challenges and your own competitive position
- *Understanding* of the new definition of quality and of the role of quality in the success of your company
- *Vision* of how good your company can really be

- *Plan* for action. Clearly define the steps you need to take to achieve your vision.
- *Train* your people to provide the knowledge, skills and tools they need to make your plan happen.
- *Support* actions taken to ensure changes are made, problem causes are eliminated and gains are held.
- *Reward and Recognize* attempts and achievements to make sure that quality improvements spread throughout the company and become part of the business plan.

Quoting Juran [14]: "For most companies and managers, annual quality improvement is not only a new responsibility; it is also a radical change in style of management—a change in culture . . . All improvement takes place project by project and in no other way."

The message is clear: (1) management has to lead the quality improvement effort, and (2) any improvement plan should consist of stepwise increments, building on experience gained in initial pilot projects, before expanding horizontally to cover all sub-processes.

A generic plan for driving a software development organization towards continuous process improvement and a case study implementation of the plan is presented in Kenett and Koenig [15] and Kenett [16]. An expanded adaptation of this plan consists of the following five steps:

1. *Define* an integrated software development process.
2. *Support* this framework with an automated development environment, where possible.
3. *Identify key areas* for process improvements.
4. Within these areas: *assign ownership*, determine metrics, create feedback loops, provide training, and establish pilot projects.
5. *Support and fortify* the continuous improvement efforts.

The first three steps should be carried out by an interdisciplinary team of experts from the various software development activities. The last two steps have to involve management and working groups centered around the main development sub-processes. Step three sees the phasing-out of the experts team and the phasing-in of improvement projects and middle management direct involvement. The whole effort requires a dedicated "facilitator" and management's commitment and leadership. The facilitator function is sometimes carried out by the SEPG (see Chapter 1). The global objective is to include every member of the software development organization, including its suppliers and customers, in the continuous process improvement effort.

2.3.3 Software Process Issues in Strategic Quality Planning

Identification of the key areas for process improvements is one of the hardest tasks concerned with process improvement. Without some sort of structure in place to accomplish this, the efforts will be diffuse, disconnected, and uncoordinated. For instance, if you bring 10 experts from the organization into a meeting and ask them to brainstorm what's needed to improve the process, more than likely, you will get something on the order of 50 to 100 ideas about what could be done. The task, then, is to make order out of chaos: how to boil this large number of ideas down into a few essential projects, with some sort of priority assigned to each.

There are various ways of bringing structure to the process. The use of an accepted model to characterize how a mature software development organization produces software is an essential element. There are a number of such models: the CMM and ISO's quality and software process standards (9000-3 and 12207) are such examples. We will discuss these in a little more detail in Chapter 3.

The CMM, as indicated in Chapter 1, has an appraisal methodology associated with it, called the CMM-Based Appraisal for Internal Process Improvement (CBA-IPI). The appraisal methodology is used to determine where an organization currently fits within the CMM. Knowing this, and knowing what practices exist or don't exist relative to the CMM, an organization can use the results of an assessment as the basis for planning and performing process improvement. It is thus a very useful device for organizations who are interested in software process improvement.

In comparison to ISO 9001 or 9000-3, the CMM can be considered to be more effective for organizations planning software process improvement. ISO 9001 or 9000-3 is effective for initially establishing a quality system. Because of the requirements for corrective action, it fosters process improvement. On the other hand, the CMM has a built-in prescription for process improvement. It specifies required practices for implementation at increasing levels of capability. For those organizations that prefer ISO standards, ISO 12207 could be used more effectively than 9000-3 for process improvement because of its coverage of topics, but it has no associated assessment methodology as yet. The determination of the degree of compliance with 12207 is, therefore, more subjective than with the CMM or any of the other ISO 9000 series of standards.

It is important to have as a starting point some effective model of how organizations develop software. With this as a starting point, comparisons can be made of the current state of the practice against the model. Long range strategic planning starts with the determination of long range objectives, for example, reaching level 3 of the CMM in four years. Having selected an effective model of how organizations improve in capability, it is then necessary to determine the current state of the practice. This involves determining deficiencies against the model and prioritization of the actions needed to eliminate the deficiencies. Many models are available, and an organization, when choosing a model, should choose one that is suitable for their marketplace. For instance, software organizations that do business in Europe will undoubtedly have to meet the requirements of ISO 9001 or 9000-3, while those in the U.S. that do business with the U.S. Government may have to meet the Level 2 or 3 requirements of the CMM. A number of U.S. businesses are now requiring their suppliers to be operating at Level 2 or 3 of the CMM. Companies like Boeing and the Norfolk and Western Railroad have required this degree of capability of their suppliers in certain cases. Other commercially-based U.S. and international companies have imposed the CMM for their own internal operations.

A final note: Measurement is an extremely important part of strategic planning. No process improvement project should be implemented unless there is some measurable pay-off for the organization. These can ultimately be related to dollars earned, but in their most apparent form, they may be perceived as reduced time to market, improved productivity (for example, in terms of source lines of code produced per developer per day), improved quality (such as reduced errors per line of code or function point in the delivered software), or improved customer satisfaction (as measured by a customer survey). In order to know if the improvement has (or will) yield positive results, an initial baseline should be established. Without that baseline, it is impossible to know if any improvement has been achieved. Many organizations do not collect even fundamental measurements, such as productivity or quality measures. For these organizations, meaningful strategic planning will be made more difficult.

2.3.4 Software Process Management Principles

Would you buy a car from a company that built them without drawings, specifications, quality control, or the like? Hardly! One can easily imagine what the quality of such a car would likely be. Yet, the world continues to buy software from companies that effectively operate in that kind of mode! To all intents and purposes, these companies are operating without a process. The significance of this reflects itself in the quality of the software they produce.

There is no need to dredge up tons of data showing that, too frequently, software is delivered late, over budget, and containing far too many errors. Horror stories demonstrating these facts abound. These problems occur because the organizations producing the software have violated the basic premise of software process management: the productivity of an organization and the quality of the products they produce are governed by the quality of the processes used. Only in recent years has there been data available to indicate a correlation between process and software product quality. In Chapter 1, data from the SEI was presented showing that for approximately 606 organizations that had had assessments performed, approximately 73.3% of these sites did not employ a defined software development process (see Figure 2.5 and Reference 17).

Process Maturity Distribution

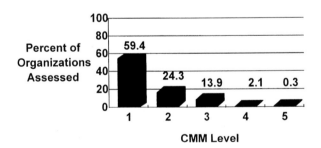

Figure 2.5 Process capability benchmarks.

This meant that no common practices were utilized (institutionalized) within these organizations, if any practices were codified at all. Where any practices may have been codified, they could vary from project to project, even though these projects were typically within the same application domain. In other words, there were no benefits gained from lessons-learned, and the organization had not as yet availed itself of the advantages that could accrue from practices that proved to be beneficial. Only 24.3% of the sites surveyed had even achieved basic management control over their projects.

Over the last 40+ years, software development has been evolving from an art form to a disciplined practice. In the early days of software development (Table 2.2), application development was almost entirely oriented toward the production of custom software, which was executed in batch mode. A user requested a program to be developed for a specific application, such as time-keeping records calculated from data on time cards, or the calculation of a trajectory using a least-squares fit of observations recorded by independent cinetheodolites or ground radars. The "requirements" for the program were worked out verbally between the primary user and the programmer. In general, no organized development process was uti-

Table 2.2   Evolution of Software Development

Time period	Software use characteristics	Software development characteristics
1950 to mid-60s	Batch processing Custom Software Limited Distribution	Single Developer/Maintainer Implicit process non-existent documentation
1960 to mid-70s	Multi-user Real-time Database Product software	Multiple Developers project teams rudimentary methodologies development as art form
1970 to mid-80s	Distributed systems microprocessor applications low-cost hardware consumer market	Rudimentary processes software tools development activity still an art form
Current decade	Client/server expert systems parallel architectures	Process focus case environments 4GLs need for flexibility

lized. Formal documentation of requirements or design was virtually non-existent. Occasionally, programmers maintained notebooks to record notes of conversations with the user and some design notes; however, the content requirements were rarely formalized, and the content varied considerably from programmer to programmer. We have evolved from that state to one today where successful, timely, cost-effective software production is heavily dependent on effective processes.

In Section 2.3.1, we defined software processes. To reiterate, software process is the total set of software engineering activities needed to transform a user's requirements into software. These include the activities, methods, practices, and transformations that are used to develop and maintain software and its associated products, i.e., documentation and code. The development and maintenance efforts consist of many such clusters of activities, methods, practices, and transformations. There are processes for developing requirements. There are processes for the production of a detailed design. There are configuration management and quality control processes. An effective process for development or maintenance of software consists of the careful linkage of these processes, such that there is an end-to-end integration of them. Each such process supports another, and facilitates the effective execution of the process. For example, configuration management supports the development of requirements by ensuring that the requirements, once established, are baselined, and that a mechanism exists to ensure the orderly management of changes to them. Quality control supports this set of activities, as well, by ensuring that reviews of the requirements for technical adequacy take place, and by auditing the configuration management process to determine if the integrity of the requirements has been compromised.

Process improvement cannot occur in a chaotic environment. If there is no attempt to characterize the current process, the situation is too labile to perform any meaningful process improvement. One needs a stable process, no matter how inefficient or cumbersome, to begin to characterize it. Why is it so necessary to characterize the process? Process improvement requires process measurement. It is impossible to control that which cannot be measured. If the process is random, ad hoc, chaotic, then the organization's activities are more like Brownian motion, making the measurement problem all the more difficult.

Juran [5] speaks of chronic waste. Chronic waste can be described as a statistical measure of the minimum expected defect rate. For a manufacturing process, the chronic level of waste can be easily illustrated by looking at, say, the production scrap rate. It can be calculated from production run to production run by calculating the mean and the standard deviation. For a statistically significant sample of production runs, the chronic level of waste would be the scrap rate with a range of 3 sigma units above and below the average. For software this can be illustrated by the following example. A number of observations are made of the defects found during a large number of code walkthroughs that were conducted for a number of projects. For the sake of discussion, let us say that the mean number of defects measured were 2 per KSLOC, and the standard deviation was 0.23. The chronic level of waste would then be 1.31 defects per KSLOC with a range of 1.31 to 2.69.

This chronic level of waste discussed above is a function of the quality of the development process used. Waste is chronic because the process was planned that way. We find that organizations that do very little quality planning will tend to produce software with high levels of chronic waste that can vary drastically from project to project. Organizations that have a well-defined process in place will tend to have lower levels of chronic waste, and more consistency in the quality of the software product from project to project. Furthermore, organizations who focus on process improvement as well, will achieve gradual lowering of their chronic level of waste.

If we want to lower the level of chronic waste, we need to know the context in which it occurs. Chronic waste provides an opportunity for improvement. Organizations that seize this opportunity are involved in process improvement.

2.3.5 The Unique Characteristics of Software Development and Maintenance Processes

Processes are easily recognized in environments with repetitive operations. For instance, a bank teller handles customer requests using a procedure that is designed to provide customers with a uniform level of service. In order to achieve this uniformity, banks typically provide employees with training programs and written material describing policies and procedures. In a second example, a machine operator who automatically inserts electronic components into printed circuit boards has a set of specifications listing requirements for the inserted components, an operator's manual to follow, a maintenance schedule to comply with, and a troubleshooting handbook to help overcome unexpected problems.

Both the bank teller and the machine operator are in charge of processes where "inputs" are transformed into "outputs." The teller satisfies a customer request using a form completed by the customer, a terminal, a printer, verbal instructions from his supervisor and what he has learned in the bank's training program. All these are inputs to the process. The teller transforms these inputs into an output or "product" that has an impact on the customer. This transformation is called a "process." The rendered service is the output. The inputs are provided by "suppliers," some internal to the bank and some external.

A key factor in improving processes is feedback. One prime source of feedback on the performance of the process is derived from simply asking the customer. This is typically done using written surveys and customer interviews. An important characteristic of processes in the service industries is that their products cannot be stored and that there is no possible inventory build-up. On the other hand, the machine operator can produce batches of circuit boards that can wait on carts or other storing devices for the next manufacturing step to begin.

The process of inserting components transforms bare circuit boards into assembled boards, ready to be soldered and tested. The feedback on the components' insertion process comes from several sources: Internal feedback from the operator's self-inspection procedure, using the specifications for the inserted components, and external feedback coming from the soldering and testing processes. These sources of feedback provide information on the degree to which the automatic insertion process meets specified requirements and internal customers' needs. Specifically the testing group can be perceived as an internal customer of the automatic insertion group.

A high percentage of error free assembled boards, when first tested, is a basic requirement of the test group. High failure rates result in "waste" consisting of high work-in-process inventory, retesting, rework activities and long production cycle times. Again, like in the bank's teller case, the process, its internal customers, and its internal suppliers are relatively easy to identify. Feedback loops can be naturally created and activated.

Characterizing the software development process requires characterizing all the sub-processes as well. The basic strategy behind a Software Quality Improvement Plan consists of:

1. Identifying the sub-processes, their inputs and outputs, their internal suppliers, and internal customers.
2. Constructing relevant feedback loops and organizational structures to induce improvements of the various software development sub-processes.

One might argue that there are no "processes" in software development since each requirement document, software module, or software version is unique. However the steps involved in their development are repetitive.

Recognizing the existence of development processes is a necessary first step towards process improvement. Like in the electronic assembly plant, inventory can pile up between sub-processes such as carts with printed circuit boards waiting to be soldered or tested. In software development the work in process inventory takes the form of software modules waiting to be integrated or new features that have to go through detailed design or coding. Processes that "do it right the first time" typically carry low levels of work in process inventory. The corollary being that high work in process levels and delays are indicators of poor performance.

2.4 SUMMARY

In this chapter, we discussed some basic concepts and principles of quality management. This was then followed by a discussion about the improvement process: problem recognition, project selection, diagnosis, preparing the people for change, implementing the solution, and maintaining the improvement. We then discussed the general principles of process management. The discussion was discussed at somewhat of a high level in order to lay the ground work for what follows in the remainder of the book: the specifics of implementing, monitoring, and measuring process improvement.

REFERENCES

1. Schulmeyer, G. Gordon. "Software Quality Assurance—Coming to Terms," in *The Handbook of Software Quality Assurance*, Schulmeyer, G. Gordon and McManus, James I., eds., New York: Van Nostrand Reinhold Company, Inc., 2nd ed., 1992.

2. Jones, T. Capers. *Applied Software Measurement*, New York: McGraw-Hill, 1991.

3. McCabe, Thomas J., and Schulmeyer, G. Gordon. "The Pareto Principle Applied to Software Quality Assurance," in *The Handbook of Software Quality Assurance*, Schulmeyer, G. Gordon and McManus, James I., eds., New York: Van Nostrand Reinhold Company, Inc., 2nd ed., 1992.

4. Government Accounting Office (GAO). Report No. GAO/NSIAD-91-190, "U.S. Companies Improve Performance Through Quality Efforts," May 1991.

5. Juran, Joseph M. *Making Quality Happen*, Juran Institute, 1991.

6. Dobbins, James. "The Cost of Quality," in *The Handbook of Software Quality Assurance*, Schulmeyer, G. Gordon and McManus, James I., eds., New York: Van Nostrand Reinhold Company, Inc., 2nd ed., 1992.

7. Kubler-Ross, Elisabeth. *On Death and Dying*, New York: Macmillan Co., 1969.

8. Government Accounting Office (GAO). Report No. FGMSD-80-4, "Contracting for Computer Software Development: Serious Problems Require Management Attention to Avoid Wasting Additional Millions," November 9, 1979.

9. Government Accounting Office (GAO). Report No. IMTEC-89-36, "Automated Information Systems: Schedule Delays and Cost Overruns Plaque DoD Sysytems."

10. Jones, Capers T. "Process Assessment and Software Risks," *Cross-Talk*, Software Technology Support Center, Nov. 1992.

11. Humphrey, Watts S. *Managing the Software Process*, New York: Addison-Wesley, 1989.

12. Juran, Joseph M. *Juran on Leadership for Quality: an Executive Handbook,* The Free Press, 1989.

13. Godfrey, A.B. "Buried Treasures and Other Benefits of Quality," *The Juran Report*, No. 9, Summer 1988.

14. Juran, Joseph. *Juran on Planning for Quality,* New York: MacMillan, 1988.

15. Kenett, R.S. and Koenig S. "A Process Management Approach to Software Quality Assurance," *Quality Progress*, pp. 66–70, November 1988.

16. Kenett, R.S. "Managing a Continuous Improvement of the Software Development Process," *Proceedings of the Annual Conference on Quality Improvement*, IMPRO 89, Juran Institute, Inc., 1989.

17. "Process Maturity Profile of the Software Community 1997 Update," Software Engineering Measurement and Analysis Team, Software Engineering Institute, Carnegie Mellon University, October 1997.

18. Jones, T. Capers, *Patterns of Software Systems Failure and Successes,* Boston: Thomson International Computer Press, 1996.

3

ISO 9000, SEI Capability Maturity Model (CMM), and Continuous Software Process Improvement

3.1 ISO STANDARDS

In the previous chapter, we discussed general principles of process management and continuous process improvement. We amplified the discussion with examples of how these principles are applied to software organizations. In this chapter, we will describe the application of these principles to software organizations in more detail, illustrating concrete methodologies that can be implemented. We begin by discussing standards developed and adopted by the International Organization for Standardization (ISO) located in Geneva, Switzerland.

There are a number of ISO Standards which are applicable to software development, acquisition, maintenance, and quality. These are ISO 9001, ISO 9000-3, and the emerging ISO 12207 and SPICE standards. Many organizations implement these standards in order to be registered with ISO as being compliant with one or more of their various standards. There are good business reasons for doing so. In many parts of the world, registration as being compliant with one or a number of ISO standards is essential in order to conduct business in these countries. Duly-authorized representatives of ISO conduct audits of organizations to determine their compliance.

ISO 9001 is a quality system standard which is applicable to the design, manufacturing, installation, test, and maintenance of systems, typically under a two-party agreement. The text of the requirements of ISO 9001 are very much hardware system oriented.

As a consequence, they are sometimes considered to be somewhat difficult to apply to software. Consequently, the need arose to develop a guide on the application of these requirements to software. The guide is ISO 9000-3. Nonetheless, some organizations utilize 9001 as the basis for developing their software quality system, rather than 9000-3.

ISO 9000-3 is a guidebook on applying the requirements of ISO 9001 to software development and maintenance organizations, and not a software quality system standard. It describes a number of elements that should be included in an organization's quality system for software. These are organized into three major areas: framework, life-cycle activities, and supporting activities. Examples of these elements include:

- Establishment of a Quality Program (framework)
- Corrective Action (framework)
- Contract Review (life-cycle activities)
- Development Planning (life-cycle activities)
- Design and Implementation (life-cycle activities)
- Maintenance (life-cycle activities)
- Configuration Management (supporting activities)
- Quality Records (supporting activities)
- Measurement (supporting activities)

For the most part, ISO 9000-3 and ISO 9001 specify only minimal requirements for the elements covered in these standards. Effectively, they require that the organization has a quality system and a quality plan that addresses these elements, and that the organization specifies what practices it will apply in implementing these elements. Furthermore, there is a requirement that an organization be audited as part of the registration process. Periodic follow-up audits are conducted every six months subsequent to the initial registration to maintain the registration. Registered organizations must, therefore, demonstrate continuous compliance with their quality system documentation. Through the corrective action element of the standards, process improvement is addressed, although somewhat indirectly.

In essence, establishing compliance to the ISO standards plays a role in strategic quality planning. Registration is a lengthy process, involving the establishment of quality plans, procedures, etc. Preliminary audits may be used as a means of determining the readiness for registration. The process of registration can take from one to two years from the date of inception to accomplish.

Another ISO standard, called SPICE (Software Process Improvement Capability dEtermination), is nearing completion. It is similar, in some respects, to the CMM in that it has an organization of maturity levels with defined key processes. It also has an assessment methodology associated with it, which will be in the public domain. In its current form, the key process areas are selectable. Each software development organization is free to define which key processes they wish to be evaluated against.

SPICE is currently undergoing Phase 2 field trials. Formal release of SPICE is expected sometime in 1998.

The CMM, by contrast, when compared to most of the ISO standards, is fairly prescriptive. As we will see in the next section, for each Key Process Area (KPA), the Key Practices define *what* practices the organization must be performing in order to have that KPA under control. The Key Practices don't define *how* things should be done—only *what*. This leaves the organization free to choose whatever methodologies makes sense for the particular types of applications they produce. For example, for the Level 2 Software Project Planning KPA, one of the Key Practices requires the development organization to establish a software life cycle with predefined stages of manageable size for each project. There is nothing that mandates a waterfall model or a spiral model or incremental development, etc. In fact, at Level 2, each project is free to utilize a different development cycle model, just as long as one is specified.

When compared to the requirements of ISO 9000-3, the CMM is definitely more prescriptive. The same is true if we compare it to the degree of rigor specified in ISO 12207. ISO 12207 is a software life cycle standard. It tends to be somewhere between ISO 9001 (or ISO 9000-3) and the CMM in its extent of specificity. ISO 12207 tends to cover many of the same kinds of items included in the CMM. Like the comparison to 9000-3, the CMM has many areas of overlap with 12207, but there are also many areas that are unique to both standards. For instance, because 12207 is a life cycle standard, it covers maintenance more effectively than does the CMM. But the CMM does a more thorough job in covering specific software development practices (the "*whats*") that organizations should implement.

3.2 THE SOFTWARE ENGINEERING INSTITUTE'S CAPABILITY MATURITY MODEL (CMM)

In 1987, the SEI published the first [1] in a series of publications [2–6] defining a Capability Maturity Model (CMM) for categorizing the capability of software organizations to develop software. The work of the SEI in defining a Capability Maturity Model and accompanying assessment methodology is an important contribution. It has promoted significant improvements in quality and productivity, and has led to large cost savings [7,8].

In Chapter 1, we briefly described the CMM to set the stage for establishing a current process status baseline, as well as for the development of a strategic plan for process improvement. Here we describe the CMM in more detail. Capability is organized in CMM into five levels (see Figure 3.1). At the Initial level (Level 1), no organized processes exist. Developers are free to utilize methods or techniques of their own choice. Basic project control is non-existent. The situation is sometimes described as chaotic and ad hoc. Software quality is more a matter of chance, and is highly dependent on the capabilities of specific individuals within the organization. Introducing high technology software tools is very risky for such an organization.

Level 2 is called the repeatable level. At this stage of maturity, development process within the organization is intuitive, rather

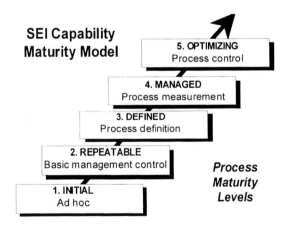

Figure 3.1   Capability maturity model.

than codified. Basic management control over projects has been achieved. Because of these factors, the organization is able to master tasks previously learned. For similar types of software projects, the organization is able to repeat past successes. That is why this stage of process maturity is labeled "repeatable." Success on development projects, however, is still very much dependent on key individuals, and not on process, because there is no organization-wide or application domain-specific codified process. In times of crisis, established procedures are abandoned, and the organization's behavior reverts back to that of a Level 1 organization. Quality is still fairly variable from project to project. Introducing technology is still a questionable practice, except to facilitate tasks and practices that have been mastered.

To reach Level 2, a software development organization must put into place basic project management practices. This includes the capability to estimate the size of the software to be produced, estimate resources (including personnel) to execute the project, and track progress against these estimates. Also included is the implementation of software configuration management and quality assurance practices. The capability to effectively manage the requirements definition process and the capability to manage subcontractors (if applicable), is also included.

Level 3 is characterized as the defined level. At this level, the organization has defined and established the software development and maintenance practices specific to the types of applications they produce. They have put into place a set of standards and procedures to codify these practices, and the organization follows them consistently. In times of crisis, the defined process is not abandoned. Training in the implementation of these practices is planned for and provided. Peer reviews are performed as in-process evaluations of product quality. There is a central focal point within the organization (sometimes called the Software Engineering Process Group, or SEPG) for overseeing the process definition (see also Section 2.1.4). The development organization is no longer highly dependent on key individuals in that the existence of a standardized process reduces the critical dependence on key individuals. At Level 3, the introduction of technology can be easily accomplished, because the organization will use it to facilitate the implementation of the defined process. (Issues concerning the introduction of technology are also under the purview of the SEPG). Quality variability is now significantly reduced. Software product quality is consistent from project to project. A Level 3 organization may not necessarily be producing the highest quality software, but it now has the wherewithal to start focusing on improving process quality.

Above Level 3, the focus of the organization now shifts from building an infrastructure to achieve consistent product quality to establishing an infrastructure to improve process quality. Recall from the principles of process management that the quality of a software product is dependent on the quality of the process used to develop it. At Level 4, the managed level, the organization is now focused on establishing a set of process measures, validating them, collecting a data base of these measures, and begins to use them to implement process corrective action, as applicable. Once these measures have been established and codified, the organization is now ready to begin to use these measures to implement continuous process improvement. At Level 5, the optimizing level, these measures are not only being used to improve existing processes, they are also being used to evaluate candidate new processes. In addition, they are being used as the basis for determining the efficacy of introducing new technologies into the organization. The process for a Level 5 organization can be characterized as mature (see Figure 3.2).

The description of the CMM, above, implies an underlying structure: specific practices have to be in place at each level above Level 1 to indicate that the organization has achieved that level.

The specifics of that underlying structure were only hinted at in the first version of the model [1–4], referred to as the "process maturity model." A clearly defined infrastructure (Figure 3.3) of maturity level, Key Process Area (KPA), Key Practices, and Subpractices was established in Version 1.1 of the CMM, released in February 1993 [5,6]. What was implied in the original version of the model was now explicitly codified in the CMM: at each maturity level, there are a number of KPAs. The KPAs are considered to be the essential

- **Defined and documented**
- **Well controlled**
- **Measured**
- **Focused on process improvement**
- **Supported by technology**

Figure 3.2   Characteristics of a mature process.

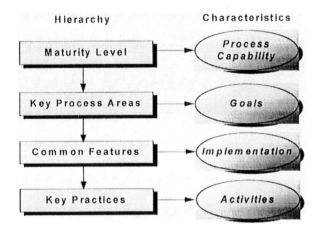

Figure 3.3 CMM organization.

building blocks for each level of the CMM. Each of these are comprised of a set of Key Practices, organized into five common features: Commitment to Perform, Ability to Perform, Activities Performed, Measurement and Analysis, and Verifying Implementation. For many Key Practices, one or more Subpractices may exist.

To reach any level N above Level 1, the organization must have implemented all the KPAs that are unique to that level, plus all the KPAs that are specific to the N-1 level. Table 3.1 describes the KPAs associated with each maturity level.

How is this framework used in practice? First, its structure provides a road map for any organization to achieve process improvement. The Key Process Areas are organized in a logical sequence that permits an organization to achieve process improvement in an orderly manner. The description of the Key Practices within each KPA identify for the organization what practices have to be in place in order to have satisfied that KPA.

A second benefit is the software process assessment, which is based on the CMM. It allows for an objective appraisal of the organization's process infrastructure to determine the degree of process capability achieved by the organization.

We will now turn to the road map and assessment aspects of the CMM in more detail.

Table 3.1 Key Process Areas

Level	Key process areas	Description
1	None	
2	Requirements management	The process of establishing, maintaining, and controlling a common understanding between the customer and the developers as to the system requirements affecting the software to be developed
	Software project planning	The process of estimating the size of the software to be developed and estimating and obtaining corresponding resource requirements in terms of costs, schedule, and staffing to support the effort
	Software project tracking and oversight	The process of tracking and reviewing the project against the estimated resource requirements, and applying corrective action, as necessary
	Software subcontract management	The process of selecting a subcontractor, establishing a commitment to perform, and surveilling the subcontractor's activities against commitments
	Software configuration management	The process of applying identification schemes to software products, controlling changes to the products, and maintaining an audit trail for all versions and changes
	Software quality assurance	The process of verifying that products and processes comply with requirements and work standards
3	Organization process focus	The implementation of a resource for maintaining cognizance over the organization's process, including the development, maintenance, assessment, and improvement of them

	Organization process definition	The activity of institutionalizing the process, and providing for the assets (for example, standards and procedures) to implement it
	Training program	The provisioning of training for the organization to provide current and future necessary skill sets
	Integrated software management	The integration of management and software engineering practices into a coherent process
	Software product engineering	The utilization of the defined process in the activity of developing and maintaining the software
	Intergroup coordination	The integration of the software engineering organization's activities with all other project organizations to implement system level requirements and objectives
	Peer reviews	The implementation of in-process reviews with peers of the developers to remove defects at the earliest possible stages of the development process
4	Quantitative process management	The establishment of a database of process measures to use as a means of maintaining process capability
	Software quality management	The quantitative determination of product quality and assessment of these values against quality goals
5	Defect prevention	The process of identifying causes of defects and prevention of their occurrence
	Technology change management	The evaluation of candidate new technologies for suitability in terms of process improvement
	Process change management	The process of reducing the chronic level of waste

3.2.1   Key Process Areas as Road Maps

As Figures 3.1 and 3.3 indicate, the maturity level indicates process capability. The extent of that capability is indicated by the Key Process Areas contained within each maturity level. Each KPA indicates goals for the organization to achieve in improving their process capability. For example, for the Software Project Planning KPA, the goals are [6]:

- Software estimates are documented for use in planning and tracking the software project
- Software project activities and commitments are planned and documented
- Affected groups and individuals agree to their commitments related to the software project

The goals then become the basis for the Key Practices associated with the KPA. The goals are accomplished across all projects within the affected organization by institutionalizing them, i.e., there is a methodology established for accomplishing the Key Practices, which is codified in the form of standard practices within the organization. Naturally, as the organization matures, i.e., improves in their process capability, the scope and extent of the standard practices will expand.

The Key Practices are organized by Common Features, which are common attributes of the KPAs. The Common Features and their descriptions are indicated below:

Common feature	Description
Commitment to perform	This is an indicator of the organizations intent to perform the activities subsumed by the KPA. For this to occur, there must be policies in existence requiring the performance of these activities, plus senior management backing.
Ability to perform	This is an indicator of the extent to which resources, infrastructure, and training exist in the organization to enable personnel to perform the necessary activities.
Activities performed	This indicates the actual performance of the necessary practices. These include the planning, performing, and tracking of the activities, as well as any necessary corrective actions to them.

| Measurement and analysis | This encompasses measurement of the process and analysis of the measurements to determine the effectiveness of the Activities Performed. |
| Verifying implementation | This is, effectively, a quality assurance activity, i.e., audits and reviews to verify that the required activities are being performed in compliance with the established process. |

Within each of the Common Features, a set of Key Practices exist. They are the activities that the organization performs within each KPA. The Activities Performed Key Practices are the activities that the organization actually performs in implementing the KPA. The activities in the other four Common Features are in the nature of providing an infrastructure in that:

- The Commitment to Perform Key Practices are the commitments that have to be made in order to signify to the organization that the process is to be implemented,
- The Ability to Perform Key Practices define the assets and resources that have to exist in order to implement the KPA,
- The Measurement and Analysis Key Practices are the measurements that have to be performed in order to determine how well the KPA is functioning, and
- The Verifying Implementation Key Practices are the verifications that are performed to verify that all the Key Practices in all the Common Features are being performed as prescribed.

The Subpractices amplify the Key Practices. They describe more specifics of what the organization must do to implement the Key Practice. For instance, in the Software Quality Assurance KPA, under the Ability to Perform Common Feature, Ability 2 (a Key Practice) states [6]:

Adequate resources and funding are provided for performing the SQA activities.

The Subpractices for this Key Practice indicate what is required for this ability to exist.

1. A manager is assigned specific responsibilities for performing the project's SQA activities.

2. A senior manager, who is knowledgeable in the SQA role and who has the authority to take appropriate oversight actions, is designated to receive and act on software non-compliance items. All managers in the SQA reporting chain to the senior manager are knowledgeable in the SQA role, responsibilities and authority.

3. Tools to support the SQA activities are made available.

In this manner, the road map for achieving process improvement is provided. Level by level, KPA by KPA, a set of Key Practices are defined, together with the pointers to indicate how the Key Practice is to be implemented. It is strongly recommended that the reader who is seriously interested in process improvement study the material in References 5 and 6. They provide the building blocks for a sensible, orderly strategy for achieving process improvement.

3.2.2 The CMM as an Assessment Tool

Recall from Chapter 2 that one of the primary principles of process change is the necessity to understand the current process first before improvement can be effectively introduced. There is an old Chinese proverb that says, "If you don't know where your are going, any road will do." Watts Humphrey has a corollary to that which says, in essence, "If you don't know where you are, a road map won't help." An assessment is a tool which enables organizations to understand the current process—to determine where on the map the organization is. It makes a great deal of sense to perform an assessment using the same framework by which the organization bases its strategy for process improvement. In other words, if an organization uses the CMM as the model for process improvement, it should also make a determination where the organization currently stands with respect to that model.

The SEI methodology for determining where an organization stands relative to the CMM, called the CMM-Based appraisal for Internal Process Improvement (CBA-IPI), is a self-appraisal by an organization that surveys a cross-section of that organization to determine what development or maintenance practices are currently employed. It is often vendor-assisted, utilizing a vendor trained in the assessment methodology that has an authorization from the SEI to lead assessments. Some of the larger software development organizations have a few of their own personnel authorized to lead assessments. Under these circumstances, these organizations do not need a vendor to lead the assessment.

Many organizations have the mistaken impression that the assessment is nothing more than responding to a Maturity Questionnaire. While responses to a questionnaire will provide useful information, it will not help the organization focus in on the most critical issues facing it. The assessment methodology itself facilitates that.

To begin, an assessment clearly requires management commitment. There is an investment of time and money on the part of the organization. If management is ambivalent about implementing process improvement, it is better not to begin an assessment at all. The assessment process tends to raise hopes within the organization that improvement will occur. If that is not to be, it then becomes more demoralizing to the organization to undergo an assessment and have no improvement occur than not to assess at all.

The assessment process, as discussed below, describes the way that an assessment would be performed for a large software organization. For smaller organizations, the process is tailored to accommodate the size of the organization, thus requiring a smaller commitment of personnel and time.

An assessment is performed by a team of vendor and client organization personnel. The assessment is led by the vendor, but the team includes senior personnel from the client. Prior to the assessment, planning for the assessment and training is performed by the vendor. An assessment team is comprised of, generally, two vendor participants, and three to six client participants. The training session includes the features and significance of the CMM and the assessment techniques. This enables the client team members to fully perform all assessment activities necessary to distill out a set of findings from the assessment process. At the conclusion of the training, planning for the actual on-site assessment period is then begun. This includes planning the logistics of the assessment, the selection of the projects that will be considered during the assessment, as well as selection of the representatives from the functional areas who will participate in group discussions. The projects are represented by their project leaders, i.e., the individual who has responsibility for meeting schedule and budget for the project, as well as the technical adequacy of the delivered product. The functional area representatives (or FARs as they are referred to) are senior people (typically, about 10 years of experience) who are performing non-management roles in disciplines such as requirements analysis, design, test, configuration management, etc. They should be people who are well respected in the organization and are opinion leaders. They should not be people who are dispensable within the organization or who stifle discussion. The FARs include personnel from the projects undergoing the appraisal as well as individuals from other projects.

An assessment will typically include three to five projects as part of the assessment, although assessments have been conducted where only one project was considered and as many as six were included. It is preferable to select projects that are at various points in the life cycle, e.g., one that has just started, one or more that are in the middle of the life cycle (such as coding or unit-level testing), and one that is nearing the end of the development effort. Maintenance projects can also be selected. It is also good to have a mix of developer experience from project to project, as well as a mix of higher order languages used by the projects. The selection of the projects and functional area representatives must be coordinated with management in order to obtain management commitment for their participation. Table 3.2 indicates typical commitment requirements for assessment participants. For smaller organizations, the tailored process would require fewer hours from the team members, but about the same number of hours for the rest; however, the

Table 3.2 Assessment Participant Commitment Requirements for a Typical Level 1 Organization

Function	No. of hours
Each assessment team member (except site coordinator)	112
Site coordinator	128
Assessment participants	
managers	8
project leaders	8
functional area representatives	8
Senior management	8
Secretarial support	10
Other support	10

smaller organization will need to provide fewer project leaders and functional area representatives.

A major principle underlying the assessment concerns confidentiality. Strict confidentiality is observed. This is essential in order to conduct an effective assessment. Much information is divulged that could have an adverse effect on the careers of the participants, if mishandled by managers or supervisors who feel threatened by the process. Consequently, findings are presented as composite findings that pertain to the organization as a whole. There is no attribution to specific projects or individual workers. The assessment team and participants agree to keep all information confidential. Some data from the assessment is sent to the SEI to allow the SEI to perform statistical analysis; however, the SEI is also bound by the confidentiality requirement. They only reveal composite results, with no attribution to specific organizations, individuals, or projects. Individual organizations, on the other hand, are free to publicly discuss the results of the assessment, if they choose. Even in doing this, there is never any reference to individuals or specific projects, since this was never revealed to the organization to begin with.

About a week or so before the on-site period begins, an assessment participants briefing is held. The purpose of that meeting is to apprise the participants of the assessment, the purpose of it, the principles underlying it, the roles they will perform, and the commitment expected of them. Prior to this meeting, the client organization's management should have coordinated with the participants to ensure their availability and willingness to participate in the assessment. At the conclusion of the briefing, the project leaders are administered a Maturity Questionnaire. The team members then meet (after the questionnaires have been completed) to review the answers and determine specific issues to discuss with the project leaders.

The actual assessment is a highly intense activity that occurs over an extended period that can last from five to ten days, depending on the size of the organization and the CMM level at which the organization believes it is functioning. It includes not only the team members from the client, but, as indicated before, also requires limited participation by project leaders from selected projects, middle managers, and selected senior technical specialists. Prior to the start of the so-called On-Site Period, the team will begin the assessment process by performing an evaluation of pertinent documentation. The purpose of this evaluation is to determine the existence of:

- Policies requiring the performance of practices specified by the CMM
- Standards and procedures
- Work products required by the standards and procedures, such as Software Development Plans, requirements specifications, design descriptions, test plans, etc.
- Reports of audits conducted to determine compliance with specified policies and processes

These artifacts are evidence that the organization has established a process, is committed to it, is providing the necessary resources, and is following it. The above list is only an example of the types of documents that this part of the assessment covers. As the document evaluation progresses, data consolidation is performed, and some tentative findings begin to emerge.

On the first day of the so-called On-Site Period, the proceedings are sometimes kicked off by a charge to the participants from the senior manager, which is effectively a pep talk. This is done to indicate to the participants that senior management is backing the assessment and the whole concept of process improvement. This is then followed by discussions with the project leaders. Based on the analysis of the responses to the questionnaire, open-ended questions are asked of the project leaders to obtain a clearer picture of the practices they employ on their projects. The purpose of this session is to obtain a sense of what practices are employed, from the perspective of the project leaders, and to what extent they are institutionalized across the organization.

The project leader sessions are then followed by open-ended discussion sessions with the FARs. These sessions are organized in reverse life cycle order with personnel whose major activities occur during discrete phases of the development cycle. For instance, the first group of FARs is typically those who are associated with release (for example, configuration management personnel) and quality assurance for the deliverable product. The next group is typically the group responsible for software integration and test. They are followed by a group responsible for coding and unit-level testing, and the final group is responsible for requirements and design. These people are invited to discuss anything they want to about how the software development process is conducted. They can talk about the good, as well as the bad. No specific questions are asked of them, except to obtain clarification of remarks made. The content of these sessions is sometimes augmented through asking the FARs some of the same questions that were asked of the Project Leaders. This is done to explore specific areas that are in question. Through this technique, many of the problems the organization is experiencing are brought to the surface. Since the FARs attend in reverse life cycle order, the problems they discuss are generally the problems that they feel are dumped in their laps because of the process problems that have occurred in the previous phases of the activity. It is also possible to begin to see if any commonality of problems are brought up between the FARs and the project leaders.

In addition to the discussion with the FARs, a discussion is also held with the middle managers. This is done for three purposes: (1) obtain the process perspective of the middle managers, (2) obtain confirmation of the process and organizational problems raised by the FARs, and (3) obtain buy-in for the assessment and process improvement efforts from the middle managers. Sometimes, an interview will be scheduled with the senior manager, as well. We often find that the senior manager feels left out of the assessment process. This interview helps provide valuable information and make the senior manager feel part of the process.

During the days that the interviews and discussions are held, data consolidation continues. Additional tentative conclusions are reached. Sometimes, the need to look at additional documentation emerges to fill in some informational gaps. The documentation is identified, obtained, and reviewed in order to supplement the information that has already been obtained.

Following the conclusion of the discussion/interview sessions, the assessment team meets to develop a preliminary set of findings. These are organized into a draft set of final findings, which identifies specific findings based on the CMM, as well as pertinent non-CMM findings, such as organizational issues inhibiting the ability to implement effective process improvement. The findings are typically organized by Key Process Area, indicating strengths, weaknesses, and sometimes the consequences of the weaknesses. A dry run of the draft final findings is presented, in turn, to the assessment team, FARs, project leaders, and middle managers. Feedback is accepted from each group. If there is any strong disagreement with any of the findings, that finding is eliminated. The intent is to obtain consensus among all the participants on the findings, and strong disagreement negates consensus. The final findings briefing to senior management is drafted based on the feedback received.

At the conclusion of the On-Site Period, a presentation of findings is then made to senior management. Senior management attendance at the briefing is essential, again, to indicate their support of the assessment and process improvement.

Following the On-Site Period, a set of recommendations are drawn up, and then an action plan is developed to implement the recommendations. These, too, are presented to senior management. The development of the recommendations and the action plan may sometimes be facilitated by the vendor. The vendor is also available to assist client companies in implementing their action plans.

A more detailed discussion of the formulation of the action plan is found in the next section.

3.3   IMPLEMENTING SOFTWARE PROCESS IMPROVEMENT

Implementing software process improvement involves the development of an overall strategy. Process improvement does not occur overnight, and can not be implemented on a "fad of the week" basis. If it is, it is doomed to failure. Process improvement requires patience on the part of all parties involved: management, the developers, and the stakeholders. Many small steps are involved in process improvement. The first, and most crucial step, is committing to process change. There has to be an acknowledgment by all parties that process improvement is required in order to remain competitive. Accompanying that acknowledgment must be a willingness on the part of management to commit the necessary resources to accomplish rational process change.

3.3.1   Developing a Long-Range Action Plan for Process Improvement

In Chapter 2, we spoke of the improvement process, and the fact that the process transitions through several steps. The first step is problem recognition. This may be accomplished by performing an assessment, as described above. For purposes of our discussion, we will utilize the CMM-based appraisal methodology as the basis for obtaining a baseline from which to begin the process improvement effort. An assessment of the current state of the practice leads to a set of findings and a corresponding set of recommendations for process improvement. These become the basis for selecting process improvement projects (the second step) and developing the action plan for process improvement (see Figure 3.4).

The strategy for implementing the recommendations should be addressed in a plan that accomplishes the actions as a series of small projects. The plan should identify the resources (including personnel, capital outlays, and software and hardware tools) needed to execute the projects, the schedule, associated tasks, project responsibilities, and measures that will be utilized to indicate success or failure. At the top level, we have the overall plan, which identifies and prioritizes the individual projects. Rough, order-of-magnitude costs for executing these projects are estimated, together with a schedule that shows the phasing of each of these projects. Once the long-range plan has been approved, detailed implementation plans for each of the approved projects can then be developed. These plans would contain a more refined cost estimate and schedule for performing each of the projects. Figure 3.5 illustrates the relationships.

The long-range action plan should be one that is commensurate with the overall business objectives of the organization. An approach

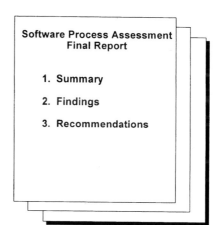

Figure 3.4 Software process assessment final report.

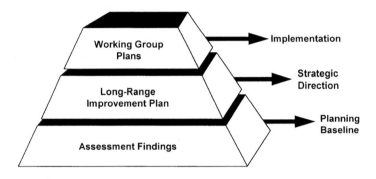

Figure 3.5   Action planning.

for developing such a plan has been developed by Frank Koch*. A description of the approach follows. Figure 3.6 illustrates the process.

In developing this plan, a team is organized consisting of the personnel who participated in the assessment, as well as any other personnel who have a vested interest in the outcome of the planning

---

* Reproduced and adapted by permission of Frank Koch, Process Strategies, Inc., Box 104, Walpole, ME, 04573-0104.

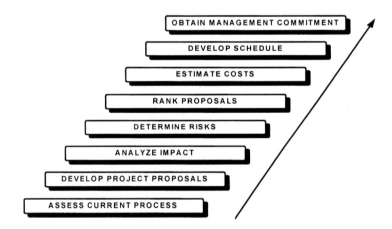

Figure 3.6   The long range action planning process.

effort. This team is the focal point for the planning process. In Chapter 2, we discussed the concept of the Quality Council. We pointed out that sometimes the role of the Quality Council is split between senior management and the Software Engineering Process Group (SEPG). Members of that Quality Council (the SEPG) will typically participate in this team. As we will show a little later, senior management also has an important role to perform. This is in keeping with the principles discussed in Chapter 2.

To expedite undertaking the various analyses that need to be performed and to achieve agreement on priorities, the planning process is typically conducted in a workshop mode, led by a facilitator.

3.3.1.1 Develop Project Proposals

The strategic direction for process improvement is set based on the recognition of an existing problem within the organization (see Section 2.2.1). The problem could be loss of market share or degraded quality in delivered software products. Some general underlying causes for the problem can be determined, by comparison against a standard benchmark. An assessment can be conducted to compare the organization's performance against this benchmark. An example of one such benchmark is the CMM. The description of the long-range planning methodology that follows is based on using the results of a CMM-based appraisal, as well as other considerations. The starting point is the assessment, to determine the current state of the practice. (The conduct of the assessment is discussed in Section 3.2.2, above). If the organization desires to improve productivity and product quality, the CMM and the assessment findings help to set the strategic direction. It identifies the Key Process Areas (KPAs) and associated key practices that must be implemented to reach that goal. Near-term priorities for accomplishing the assessment's recommendations should be based on the most critical process issues currently facing the organization; however, the priorities must be consistent with the findings of the assessment. A Level 1 organization, for instance, should not normally be addressing Level 3 issues in their action plan (unless one of them was a particular critical issue for the organization), because there are Level 2 issues that need to be addressed first. Even within the Level 2 issues, some may be a more burning issue for the organization than others.

While the CMM is one factor that helps to set the strategic

direction, other factors enter into the picture as well: alignment with the organization's business goals and risk. We will look at that further in the next section.

Based on the findings of the assessment, a set of recommended solutions to the process issues identified in the assessment report are proposed. This begins the process of project selection (see Section 2.2.2). Typically, numerous projects are proposed. Through discussions and nominal group techniques, the list is winnowed down to a manageable size: something on the order of a dozen. All of these projects cannot be implemented at once. Some sort of prioritization must occur. How this occurs is described in the next section.

3.3.1.2   Analyze Impact

In arriving at the highest priority improvement projects, three factors must be considered: impact, risk, and benefits. In Section 2.2.2, we discussed the process of project selection. This section describes a specific technique for continuing the process for arriving at a selection of specific process improvement projects for implementation.

When we look at impact, we are looking at the impact of the projects on the overall strategic business objectives of the organization. We also look at the number of KPAs affected by the project, since an action to be implemented can impact more than one KPA. For example, suppose there is a recommendation to implement configuration management to accomplish the baselining of requirements documentation and instituting change control over them. Suppose there is another recommendation concerning subcontractor management that addresses having a solidified set of requirements for the prospective subcontractors before the subcontract is let. A single project to implement a well-thought out change management process can have impact on the business objectives, as well as implementing process improvement based on both of these KPAs.

In evaluating the business impact, the beginning point is the statement of the organization's business objectives. These are then characterized by a set of critical success factors that help to determine if these objectives are being met. These should be expressed in terms that relate to the data processing or software development organization. It is best to limit this list to a maximum of about seven critical success factors (CSFs). Generally, this list, as it relates to the data processing or software development organization, is developed in a joint session consisting of the cognizant senior management and the members of the planning team. If the business objectives have already been clearly and publicly stated by management in some documented form, the focus is then on the development of the CSFs. Sometimes, we find that the business objectives have not been articulated for the organization, and the first order of business then becomes to state those. The intent of the activity is to reach consensus on the CSFs affecting the software development organization, and to establish weights for each of the factors. It is also the intent to enlist senior management participation in this activity, thus establishing their commitment to the process improvement activity. Recall from Chapter 2 that senior management active involvement is essential for institutionalizing process improvement (see Section 2.2.8).

A number of techniques exist to attain a consensus within a group on the CSFs and their weights. Techniques such as Australian balloting may be used quite effectively. (A discussion of these techniques is outside of the scope of this book). Each of the projects is then scored against these CSFs, in terms of how well they will support achieving them. For each project, a normalized score is calculated, which is later used for rank-ordering the projects. Figure 3.7 illustrates the process.

Process Improvement Proposal Impact Analysis for Project "C"

Critical Success Factors Description	Weight	Impact Score	Wtd. Score
CSF 1	6	5	36
CSF 2	4	1	4
CSF 3	10	9	90
CSF 4	2	6	12
CSF 5	8	4	32
TOTALS:	30		174
NORMALIZED SCORE:			5.8

Figure 3.7 Performing the impact analysis based on business objectives.

A second impact analysis is then performed, in which each of
the projects is evaluated against their impact on achieving the next
level of capability on the CMM. A simpler weighting is used here,
based on a high-low scale. Recall that some projects can impact more
than one KPA. Those KPAs that are associated with the next level
of maturity receive the highest weighting, while those that area associated with higher levels of maturity receive lower weighting. The
objective is to get to the next higher level of maturity. Accordingly, as
a first cut, all KPAs at the next level of maturity receive the identical
(higher) rating, while the KPAs at the next level of maturity receive
an identical lower rating. The project is then scored against each of
the affected KPAs, and a project normalized score is calculated, as
previously described. As a refinement, a second cut at the impact
analysis may be performed. At the next level of maturity, some KPAs
may be more important than others, based on the assessment findings. The issues that are presented as assessment findings have
been identified by consensus, and reflect the most pressing issues
for the organization. Accordingly, the KPAs associated with those
issues will receive higher weighting. As before, weightings are established in a consensus gathering session, again using techniques such
as Australian balloting. Figure 3.8 illustrates the process. In performing this analysis, keep in mind that the cumulative sum of the
weighted scores for a given KPA across all projects cannot exceed

Process Improvement Proposal Impact Analysis for Project "C"			
Key Process Area KPA Weight		Impact Score	Wtd. Score
Project Planning	6	9	54
Project Oversight	6	7	42
Requirements Mgmt.	6	2	12
SQA	6	1	6
Config. Mgmt.	6	1	6
Integ. Proj. Mgmt.	2	5	10
TOTALS:	32		130
NORMALIZED SCORE:			4.1

Figure 3.8 Performing the impact analysis based on key process areas.

100%. The significance of a score of 100% is that the KPA is totally achieved. A score in excess of 100 means that the KPA has been more than achieved, which is not logically possible.

3.3.1.3 Analyze Risk

Risk refers to the difficulty associated with implementing the proposed plan. Is implementing the project a gamble, or are the results reasonably predictable? In determining this, a number of factors are considered, grouped into three categories: project size, structural issues, and technology (see Figure 3.9).

Project size, as a risk category, refers to the magnitude of the project in terms of staff-hours to implement it. In general, the smaller the number of staff-hours to perform the project, the lesser the risk.

The category of structural issues can include a number of factors, such as:

- The number of functional groups within the organization involved in the project
- The complexity of it
- The experience in the affected process domain of the people assigned to develop the solution. Are the people assigned to develop the solution novices in this area?
- The experience in the affected process domain of the people who will ultimately use it. In other words, will a great deal of training be required to familiarize the users with the practices involved?

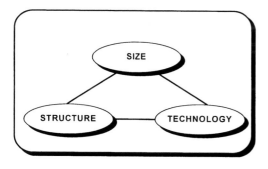

Figure 3.9 Project risk categories.

- The anticipated resistance of the organization to change in this area

The category of technology issues can includes factors, such as:

- The maturity of the proposed process within the software engineering discipline. Is the project attempting to implement a cutting edge solution?
- The availability of training in using the new methodology
- The complexity of tools or other aids that will be acquired to implement the solution
- The maturity of the tools and other aids. Is the organization going to acquire Version 1.0 of the tool (which is always a risky proposition)?
- Experience in the use of the tools or aids. How experienced are the users with the tools or aids used to support this process?

The risk evaluation is performed in a manner similar to that of the impact analysis. In the case of risk, however, a tailored set of risk factors is defined. The list of risk factors shown here are a generic list. The risk factors shown here may be not all be applicable for some organizations. Other, additional factors may be. The list needs to be refined for each organization to be applicable to that organization's specific environment.

For each project, a score is determined for each of the risk factors, based on guidelines (see Table 3.3), and a normalized score is calculated, based on the sum of the weighted scores for each of the factors. Note that there is one major difference. In the case of the impact analysis, the greater the impact, the higher the score. In the case of risk, the higher the risk, the lower the rating. Projects with the lowest risk receive the highest score.

3.3.1.4   Rank Proposed Projects

Once the impact and risk analyses have been performed, the projects are ranked according to total score. The general equation for calculating the total score is as follows:

$$\text{Total Score} = (\text{Weight}_1)(\text{Business Objective Impact}) + (\text{Weight}_2)(\text{KPA Impact}) + (\text{Weight}_3)(\text{Risk})$$

Table 3.3 Examples of Risk Factor Scoring Guidelines

Risk factor	Parameters	Score
Project size	Less than 160 staff-hours	10
	160–400 staff-hours	5
	More than 400 staff-hours	1
No. of functional groups	1–2 groups	10
	3–4 groups	5
	More than four groups	1
Process maturity	Vintage	10
	Middle-aged	5
	Bleeding edge	1
Process developer experience with	Expert	10
this type of process	Intermediate	5
	Beginner	1
Complexity of tools for supporting	Simple	10
process	Moderate	5
	Very	1
Resistance to change	Minimal	10
	Somewhat	5
	High	1

where the impacts and the risk for each project are the normalized scores developed in the manner described in the paragraphs above, and weights 1, 2, and 3 are determined by consensus. To illustrate how the rankings are developed, some organizations may consider all three items of equal importance. Under those circumstances, the equation would reduce to:

$$\text{Total Score} = (\text{Business Objective Impact})$$
$$+ (\text{KPA Impact}) + (\text{Risk})$$

Another organization might consider the business objective impact three times more important than KPA impact, and risk twice as important as KPA impact. Under those circumstances, the equation would reduce to:

$$\text{Total Score} = 3(\text{Business Objective Impact})$$
$$+ (\text{KPA Impact}) + 2(\text{Risk})$$

Each proposed project is thus scored, in turn. A tentative ranking is now established on the basis of the scores recorded for each project, with the project achieving the highest score ranking the highest. A further refinement of the ranking is then made after the conclusion of the next step.

A cost-benefit analysis (for example, return on investment) is not likely to be performed by organizations to support the ranking process. As a rule, Level 1 and 2 organizations will be unable to accurately forecast tangible benefits to be achieved from the improvement projects. These organizations typically will not have collected the data and metrics to support such projections. Such analyses are feasible for Level 4 and 5 organizations, and may likely be achievable for Level 3 organizations, or organizations close to Level 3.

3.3.1.5   Estimate Cost and Schedule

After the proposals are ranked, the next step is estimating the schedule and cost for each project by itself. In this step, the intent is not to develop fine-grained costs or schedules, but to get an overall rough order-of-magnitude estimate, in order to get an general idea of what the commitments would be for each project. Knowing the staffing and financial resources available for the near-term (for example, the remainder of the fiscal year), the team can then identify the candidate projects for the near-term plan, based on priority and available resources. Figure 3.10 illustrates the methodology. Considering the

Process Improvement Cost Summary				
Rank	Project	Cost	Cumulative Cost	
1	Project A	$23,000	$23,000	
2	Project F	55,000	78,000	Available
3	Project D	100,00	178,000	Funding
4	Project C	62,000	240,000	Level =
5	Project E	15,000	255,000	$185,000
6	Project B	37,000	292,000	

Figure 3.10   Defining the candidate projects.

fact that the projects have been prioritized, and, in all likelihood, there will be interdependencies between them, the next step is to develop an overall strategic schedule for all the projects which reflects their priorities and interdependencies. Figure 3.11 is an example of such a schedule. It is an example of a schedule for calendar year 1994, showing that the projects overlap two fiscal years, and the output from Project E becomes an input for Project B, which, as the plan indicates, would be performed in calendar year 1995. Also, the schedule indicates that Projects B and F become inputs to Project D. Consequently, the priority of the projects can change as a result of the interdependencies between projects. Projects A, F, and B may now become the projects recommended for the first year.

Another consideration is impact and visibility. For low Level 1 organizations, management may not have much credibility where it relates to process improvement. Past experience may prove that management "talks the talk," but doesn't "walk the walk." Considering that, a short term project having low risk, high visibility, and some non-trivial benefits, may be a better candidate for a high priority, initial project, even though it may have had a much lower ranking.

3.3.1.6 Obtain Management Commitment

The next step is to formalize the plan and present it to management to obtain their concurrence and commitment. Earlier, we spoke of

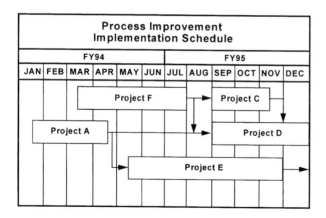

Figure 3.11 Scheduling the projects.

the necessity for senior management involvement in order to institutionalize process improvement (see also Section 2.2.8). We spoke of this in relation to their participation in the generation of the critical success factors. Once again, their participation is necessary, this time in approving the strategic plan and authorizing the initiation of the first process improvement projects.

The overall plan for process improvement is prepared and presented to the steering committee, which includes senior management. We spoke of this in Section 2.1.4, when we described the function of the Quality Council. Figure 3.12 illustrates the typical content of the plan. There would be an introductory section in the plan that would explain the purpose of the plan, describe the methodology utilized in developing the content, and briefly summarize the findings and recommendations contained in the assessment report. (It would refer the reader back to the assessment report for more detail concerning the findings and recommendations). The project descriptions are each contained in a one- or two-page summary (see Figure 3.12) that identify the project, provide a brief description of it, describe the expected benefits, identify the personnel who will be responsible for performing the project, identify the costs and associated resources, and define the duration of the project. In the description of the project will be an identification of how the process will change. It will identify the methods that will be investi-

Figure 3.12 Example of a process improvement proposal.

gated, address implementation in a trial application, identify the effort required to establish a set of trial standards and procedures, training of the personnel in the trial application in the new methods, incorporation of feedback into the methods and trial standards and procedures, and re-trial, if necessary. The estimated costs will account for these activities. This plan, after review and approval by the steering committee, is signed by them, signifying their concurrence and commitment to providing the personnel and other resources. Once the strategic plan has been approved, the detailed plans for the individual projects are then developed.

In Section 2.1.4, we also spoke of the SEPG and its relation to the Quality Council. The SEPG is the focal point for implementation of process improvement and for managing change within the organization. Typically, it will be the responsibility of the SEPG to coordinate and manage the implementation of the action plan. They should track each project against its planned schedule, funding, and task performance. Most project plans will require a pilot application of the change in the process. Once the trial application has shown that the new methods will work, the SEPG then becomes responsible for communicating this to the organization as a whole, providing education and training to the organization at large in the new methods, and promulgating the standards and procedures necessary to implement them. Senior management is also involved in this process, as well. Senior management, acting as a steering committee or Quality Council, meets regularly with the SEPG to discuss progress and status. Senior management also authorizes the official roll out of the changes in the process. After a pilot application shows the efficacy of the change, and feedback from the pilot application has been incorporated into the standards, procedures, and training materials, as appropriate, the SEPG makes a report to the steering committee. The steering committee then decides if the change should be rolled out, and, if it should, provides the authorization. The steering committee also periodically reviews the status of the action plan and decides on which improvement projects to initiate next.

3.3.2 Work Environment Factors Affecting Process Improvement Plan Implementation

In developing the plan, it is important to remember that there likely are barriers to successful implementation of process improvement.

If these barriers did not exist, it is quite likely that process improvement efforts would have already been further advanced. The plan must take these barriers into account, and address the mitigation of their effect.

The next several sections discuss some of these barriers.

3.3.2.1 *Facilities*

The physical environment in which employees work can have a major impact on productivity. Studies show that the amount of floor space allocated to an employee can have significant effect on employee productivity, thus moderating the effect of other actions taken to improve productivity through process improvement. Capers Jones [10] cites a study by De Marco that showed that the productivity of people who worked in offices having 78 square feet or more were in the high quartile. On the other hand, those who had 44 square feet or less were in the low quartile. An analysis conducted by TRW on their company-funded Software Productivity Project [11] showed that the personnel productivity on this project was 42% higher than that predicted for such a project. These personnel had been supplied with private offices having 90 to 100 square feet, floor-to-ceiling walls, carpeting, sound-proofing, and chairs that were ergonomically designed. They were provided with adequate desk area, lighting, and storage. Each office had a terminal or a work station, which was networked to computers, file servers, and printers. Roughly 8% of the productivity gain was attributed to the comfort of the work environment.

In addition to the floor space, personnel require adequate shelf space for reference material, and storing other materials (even personal items) considered important by the developers. A minimum of 20 feet of shelf space is recommended [12].

Noise level also adversely affects productivity. Noise can be especially bad in facilities where partitions do not extend to the ceiling, floors are not carpeted, and/or several people share offices. If an office is shared, people dropping in to visit with an office-mate can be very distracting—especially if the conversation is not work-related. Offices with low partitions, if the office area has not been properly sound-proofed, are susceptible to all sorts of ambient noise (people walking down the corridor, hallway conversations, etc.). Even with good sound-proofing, low partitions can still allow in a fair amount of ambient noise. The positive effects on productivity and quality of providing personnel with the latest and greatest in tools, techniques, methodologies, and training can still be blunted by failing to provide an agreeable work environment.

There are other facility/environmental factors to consider, as well. These include, among other things, the availability of [12]:

- Adequate lighting. Numerous studies indicate that fluorescent lighting *lowers* productivity.
- Free parking close to the facility.
- Availability of food service and vending machines. One site with which we are familiar provides pretzels, cookies, and potato chips of various flavors free to all work areas. Because of this and other environmental considerations, this company achieves significant output from their employees, as well as a great deal of creativity.
- Wall space for notes, 10 square feet minimum. This can be in the form of cork boards, chalkboards, or whiteboards. The availability of Post-its™ (or equivalent "stickies") are a great help in note-keeping and replacing "to-do" files.

3.3.2.2 Software Tools

Software tools can be either a godsend or a hindrance, depending on if they are used, the context in which they are used, and how they are used. We sometimes find companies who do not readily acquire software tools. They are reluctant to expend the capital funds necessary to acquire such tools. To compound matters, these and other companies, when they acquire tools, are often reticent to contract for the associated training. The non-acquisition of training is treated as a cost-savings. In actuality, it is costing these organizations more by not acquiring the necessary training. Tools do not teach the user how to use them: trainers do. Without the training, the tools either go unused, or are used inefficiently. Any productivity and quality gains that could have been realized by the use of these tools are quickly negated.

Tools, and especially computer-aided software engineering (CASE) environments, hold much promise, yet, results from the use of CASE have been a mixed bag. Studies performed on the utilization of CASE tools indicate that after one year, 70% of the CASE tool acquired have become shelfware—almost totally unused by the acquiring organization. Another 25% are used by only one group within the organization, and the remaining 5% are widely used, but not to capacity [13].

Why does this situation exist? A number of reasons have been proposed, many of which revolve on the issue of organizational readiness for CASE. For example, Howard Rubin has defined a measure of organizational readiness that is based on a matching of eight organizational attributes with eight comparable tool attributes. To illustrate, one of the organizational attributes is "Applicability," i.e., the dominant work focus of the organization (for instance, new development, maintenance). The comparable tool attribute is "Work Spectrum," which reflects the extent to which the tool supports the organization's dominant work focus. A footprint of the eight attributes of the organization's readiness is plotted on a Kiviat diagram, as is the footprint of the tool's attributes. Without going into a great deal about the methodology, suffice it to say that there has to be a considerable match-up of the two footprints for the tool to be accepted and widely used by the organization [13].

In the CMM, too, the concept of organizational readiness comes into play. Until an organization has defined, established, and codified the methodology it uses for developing software, CASE tools will be of little or no value. The tools will provide more capability than the organization can assimilate or use effectively. Accordingly, organizations functioning at very low levels of process maturity are not able to realize significant benefits from CASE. Consequently, organizations who see tools as a panacea for their productivity and quality problems without addressing the basic process problems first will find that tools are an obstacle, rather than an aid, and will have wasted considerable sums of money.

3.3.2.3   Personnel Resources

In Japan, when people enter the work force, they typically stay at one company for their entire working career. Layoffs are uncommon. (Although both of these conditions are starting to change, this is still the general rule). There is a strong feeling for the group, and people work together for the good of the organization. Maintaining motivation, and having an adequate, experienced staff is much less of a problem than it is in the Western World.

In the Western World, people want to be rewarded for their

individual contributions. If they feel that they are not, they feel free to leave their employer and go to work for another. Management, on the other hand, wants to have a free hand in reducing the work force as economic conditions change. They want to be able, when they see fit, to shift personnel from project to project to balance costs, and to sometimes replace experienced personnel with less experienced personnel. (Note that management can sometimes accomplish the same economic results by process improvement, rather than by arbitrary staff reductions or sudden changes in staffing).

Some personnel like to have training. Others resist it. Some like training in disciplines related to their current jobs. Others look at training as a way of getting a better job somewhere else. Management views of training are sometimes unclear. Training is often one of the first things cut out of the budget when companies fall on hard times. The need to reduce the cost of doing business when economic downturns occur is certainly understandable; however, many companies practice cut and slash without taking a careful look at their business practices. This was alluded to in the previous paragraph. Improving business processes can often effect significant cost-savings without the necessity for cutting personnel, or drastically reducing the training programs which can result in improved staff performance. If cutting and slashing is perceived as indiscriminate, this can severely overtax the surviving staff, and cause serious morale problems.

How companies use their training budgets varies considerably. In some companies, training is sparse. Other companies provide a great deal of training. European, Japanese, and especially Indian companies provide a great deal of training—far more than that provided by companies in the U.S. Indian companies spend as much as 5% of gross revenues each year on training [15]. Some companies succeed in providing for both individual growth, as well as growth of the organization. Others provide only for growth of the organization. Still others succeed in providing the right kinds of training, but at the wrong time: either too far before training in the discipline is needed, or too late—well after the people who needed it have limped along without it.

Intelligent utilization of personnel resources are essential for process improvement. Process improvement requires motivated personnel if the process improvement effort is to be seen as something other than the fad of the week. Experienced, skilled personnel must be employed in the planning and implementation of the process improvement efforts. Training in the new skills and disciplines to be implemented must be provided. Management must be seen as being behind the effort (more on that in the next section).

Process improvement planning must take these factors into account.

3.3.2.4 Management Policies

Process improvement starts at the top. Management commitment to process improvement must exist, or no improvement will occur. Management must be in for the long haul. There has to be a recognition that process improvement takes time, and that changes will not occur overnight. If management is unable to recognize that fact, or is not willing to stay the course during the time that it takes for process improvement to take hold, it is better not to begin.

Management must provide the resources, establish the priorities, and provide encouragement for implementing process improvement. All are essential ingredients. This fact has been recognized by the SEI in the structure of the CMM. Each KPA is comprised of 5 Common Features, as described in Section 3.2.1. These are Commitment to Perform, Ability to Perform, Activities Performed, Measurement and Analysis, and Verifying Implementation. The Key Practices for each KPA are organized by the Common Features. Two Common Features, Commitment to Perform and Ability to Perform, deal with the topic of management commitment to process improvement. Commitment to Perform enumerates Key Practices that the organization must implement to indicate management's commitment to good process. They include such things as promulgating the necessary policies within the organization requiring it to perform the good practices encompassed by the KPA, and specifying management responsibility for seeing to it that the policy is consistently implemented. Ability to Perform deals with providing the necessary resources to implement the practices, such as funding and training.

In general, if these activities are not properly managed for process improvement, they can discourage the improvement efforts. Management must be willing to make capital outlays to pay for the necessary staff to oversee the process improvement efforts and to acquire the software tools and hardware associated with the process improvement projects. This does not mean that management should sign a blank check. Reasonable budgets should be established, and the projects should be required by management to live within their budgets and schedules. Priorities should be established to take care of contingencies. By setting reasonable priorities based on sound process improvement objectives, looking for "silver bullets" can be avoided. Too often, management squanders precious financial resources on software or hardware that are looked upon as quick solutions.

The foregoing assumes, of course, that management has a genuine commitment to quality. This means that schedule is not the primary motivating factor in the organization. In too many organizations, quality assurance, configuration management, and test (among other good practices) fall by the wayside when projects fall behind. Process improvement efforts will fail, and personnel will be demotivated if management is perceived as paying lip service to quality. If schedule is overriding, quality cannot be perceived as important.

3.3 MANAGING THE IMPROVEMENT PROJECTS

The improvement projects should be managed no differently than any other software project. As part of the initial action plan development, rough order of magnitude estimates are defined for each project. Prior to the start of each project, a detailed plan for that project should be drawn up. A detailed definition of the tasks to be performed should be established. Based on the task definitions, detailed estimates of the labor hours to perform the tasks should be made, together with the schedules for their performance. If possible, identify the specific individuals who should perform these tasks, since it will be essential to obtain their management's commitment for them to support the process improvement projects. They should be individuals who have specific expertise in the affected disciplines, as well as being respected within the organization. This is necessary to facilitate acceptance of the proposed changes within the organization. Establish detailed cost estimates for each task, including non-recurring costs. This could include the cost for tools, outside consultants, training, books, etc., as well as the costs for printing draft procedures, standards, training materials, and the like for the pilot projects.

In Section 2.2.5, we spoke of the structure of the process improvement projects. We addressed the need to characterize the existing process, collect measures of the current process, and analyze the data. In addition, we talked of the need for measures to determine if the process changes provide significant benefit. By doing this, we provide data essential for proper management of the improvement projects. Consequently, in developing the plans for the projects, the detailed tasks should address (among other things) the following:

- What does the current process look like? This may involve developing a model of the current process. For instance, if the process improvement project is geared toward improving the system requirements definition process, it may be very useful to develop a model of the process currently used to develop these requirements.
- What are the inputs to and outputs from the current process? How do they relate to the quality issue?
- What measures do we have or can we generate to determine the quality of the inputs and outputs?
- How are we going to collect and analyze the data?
- What changes do we need to make to the process?
- What measures do we have to collect in order to determine if the change is beneficial?

The plan should also include provisions for pilot applications of the process change, as described previously. This involves the following:

- Identifying and selecting an on-going or new development or maintenance project in which to conduct a pilot application of the change
- Producing draft standards and/or procedures to define how the process change is to be implemented in practice
- Developing and implementing draft training materials for use in training the practitioners in the required practices
- Utilizing the measures we spoke of in the previous paragraph to evaluate the efficacy of the change.
- Applying feedback and lessons learned from the pilot application for overhauling or fine-tuning the draft materials

(standards, procedures, training materials) before rollout to the organization as a whole

- Releasing the changed process to the organization-at-large, using the revised standards, procedures, and training materials

The plan, when completed, should be submitted to the SEPG for review and comment. Feedback from the SEPG review should be incorporated into the plan. When the SEPG is satisfied with the plan's content, they will then submit it to the senior management steering committee for their review and approval (see Section 2.2.8). The steering committee, when they find the plan acceptable, should provide the specific resources required. This includes identifiable budget, as well as personnel assignments. The steering committee should be the focal point for obtaining the commitment of lower level managers to provide the specific individuals identified in the plan to support the project. If the specified individual can't be allocated to the project, then a suitable substitute should be negotiated between the steering committee and the designated project leader.

The project leader should manage the performance against the approved plan. This includes managing the expenditure of funds, tracking the schedule, and tracking the performance of the tasks. Where variances exist, they should be investigated, and if corrective action is necessary, it should be implemented. The commitment of the personnel should also be monitored. Where commitments of individuals to the project are not being kept, that problem must be worked up through the chain through the SEPG to the steering committee.

Successful process improvement projects must follow the same good project management practices that any competent project manager would follow in managing a software development project.

3.4 SUMMARY

In this chapter, we elaborated on the principles discussed in Chapter 2, and described specific applications of these principles to software process improvement. We described the CMM and the application of it to the performance of software process assessments. These yield findings which become the input for the activity of strategic planning for software process improvement. A methodology was described for performing strategic planning for process improvement, one that has been used extensively and has been quite successful.

To conclude this chapter, we discussed a number of issues that can affect the implementation of change management. This was followed by a discussion on managing the process improvement projects.

In the next chapter, we will begin the discussion on applying measurement to the process improvement activities. These measures are used to establish baselines of current performance, and to measure actual improvement.

REFERENCES

1. Humphrey, W. S. "Characterizing the Software Process: A Maturity Framework," CMU/SEI-87-TR-11 (ESD-TR-87-112), June 1987.
2. Humphrey, W. S. "Characterizing the Software Process," *IEEE Software*, March 1988, pp. 73–79.
3. Humphrey, W. S. "Managing the Software Process," New York; Addison-Wesley, 1989.
4. Humphrey, W. S. and Sweet, W. L. "A Method for Assessing the Software Engineering Capability of Contractors," CMU/SEI-87-TR-23 (ESD-TR-87-186), September 1987.
5. Paulk, M. C., Curtis, W., Chrissis, M. B., and Weber, C. V. "Capability Maturity Model for Software, Version 1.1," CMU/SEI-93-TR-24 (ESD-TR-93-177), February 1993.
6. Paulk, M. C., Weber, C. V., Garcia, S. M., Chrissis, M. B., and Bush, M. "Key Practices of the Capability Maturity Model, Version 1.1," CMU/SEI-93-TR-25 (ESD-TR-91-178), February 1993.
7. Humphrey, W. S., Snyder, T. R., and Willis, R. R. "Software Process Improvement at Hughes Aircraft," *IEEE Software*, July 1991, pp. 11–23.
8. Dion, R. "Process Improvement and the Corporate Balance Sheet," *IEEE Software*, July 1993, pp. 28–35.
9. Daskalantonakis, M. K., Yacobellis, R. H., and Basili, V. R. "A Method for Assessing Software Measurement Technology," *Quality Engineering*, 3(I), 27–40 (1990–1991).
10. Interview with T. Capers Jones. *CASE Strategies*, Vol. II, No. 9, September 1990.
11. Putnam, Lawrence H. and Myers, Ware. *Measures for Excellence; Reli-*

able Software On Time, Within Budget, Englewood Cliffs, NJ: Yourdon Press, 1992.

12. Bliss, Robert. "The Other SEE," *CrossTalk,* January 1994.
13. Source: Jerry Weinberg, cited in "The 'True' Cost of 'CASE'," Presented by Howard A. Rubin, Ph.D., CASE World, Los Angeles, CA, March 20, 1990.
14. Howard Rubin, *Using "READINESS" to Guide CASE Implementation,* "CASE Trends," November/December 1990 and January/February 1991.
15. Quann, Eileen. "Training—Your Competitive Edge in the '90s," Software Technology Conference, Salt Lake City, April 1994.

4

Software Measurements Programs: Strategies and Implementation Issues

4.1 INTRODUCTION

Measurement is an integral part of the process management strategies. Chapter 3 discussed how the SEI Capability Maturity Model and the ISO 9000 standards emphasize the role of process in determining the quality of the products. In this chapter we focus on measurement of software development and maintenance processes. The topic of process measurement will be introduced in the context of organization objectives and management strategies. One or more management strategies may be used in an organization, but for process measurement to be a relevant activity, the net result should be a focus on increasing the quality and responsiveness of the organization.

Measurement ties several disciplines together, creating an environment where inputs, processes, and outputs are controlled, and improved. Measurement is a basic need of any management activity. This chapter focuses on software measurement programs in the context of the management and control of software quality. Specifically we will cover measurement of software development and maintenance processes.

During the planning phase of a new project, measurement information from prior projects may be used to estimate parameters of the new project. During the execution of the project, process and resource measures can be collected and analyzed against such estimates. As products are created, product measures are collected and analyzed, yielding product metrics. The number of open bugs, per subsystem, is an example of a product metric.

The answer to the question, "*Why Measure?*," involves several other questions such as:

- Are the software processes more productive today than last year? Less productive? Why?
- Are the software processes delivering higher quality products today than last year? Lower quality? Why?
- Are our customers more satisfied with our software processes today than they were last year? Less satisfied? Why?
- Are the software processes more reliable this year than last year? Less? Why?
- Do the software processes cost more today than last year? Less? Why?

Note that if one removes the words *software processes* from each of the questions above and insert any other business process, the questions would still apply to organizations in general. Software processes should be treated the same as other business processes. Authors such as W. Edwards Deming, J.M. Juran, and Phil Crosby have made process modeling, measurements, and the subsequent improvements key items in improving business performance. If we apply the same continuous improvement methodology to our software processes, the need to *measure* those processes becomes critical.

4.2 DEFINITIONS

The definitions for measure and metric are not consistent throughout literature and industry publications. Often the terms measure, indicator and metric are used synonymously. In this section, we define these terms as they are used in this book.

Measure: As a noun, a measure is defined as a number that assigns values on a scale. Examples may include number of errors, lines of code, or work effort. As a verb, measure means to ascertain or appraise by comparing to a standard.

Metric: There is no single universal definition of metrics. In the context of this book, a metric is a combination of two or more measures or attributes. Examples include (1) fault density, (2) Flesch readability index and (3) man-months. In evaluating a metric we can consider several characteristics. In particular, we will want the metric to be:

- *Understandable*—It must relate to some quality or characteristics that the practitioner finds meaningful and simple to understand.
- *Field tested*—It must have a proven record by other industrial organizations or proven on local pilot effort.
- *Economical*—It should be easily extracted from existing product and processes.
- *High leverage*—It should help identify alternatives that have high impact on cost, schedule, and quality.
- *Timely*—It should be available within a suitable time frame to meet the objectives of the measurement.

Measurement: Measurement is defined as the activity of computing and reporting metrics values. Comprehensive measurement activities lead to operational control that include:

- Setting of standards or goals for relevant metrics
- Computation of relevant metrics in a timely manner
- Comparison of reported metrics value with appropriate standards or goals
- Evaluation of difference to determine required action
- Periodical review of standards, metrics definition, list of required actions

4.3 MEASURES FOR SOFTWARE PROCESS CONTROL AND IMPROVEMENT

As was stated in the previous section, we measure to understand and improve processes. There are several ways to determine what to measure in an organization. The most successful way to determine what to measure is to tie the measurement program to the organizational goals and objectives.

Victor Basili of the University of Maryland developed the "Goal-Question-Metric" method for tying the measurements to the goals (Figure 4.1).

In Basili's method, you first identify the organizational goals.

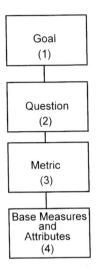

Figure 4.1 Goal-question-metric model.

This can be done by reviewing documents and by interviewing the organization's leaders. An example goal might be to "reduce time to market by 25 percent."

Once the goals are documented, a series of questions may be formulated for each goal. Example questions are "What is our current time to market?" and "What is our competitor's time to market?"

The questions then need to be analyzed to determine if a quantitative means exists to answer them. Time to market, for example, is the elapsed time, or duration, to bring a new product through the design, development, and deployment steps. Time to market analysis often must include management processes, which may also include an analysis of performance and quality.

Once the metrics are decided upon, the underlying measures must be selected and collected.

The Goal-Question-Metric is one approach. Measurement programs for software processes come in all shapes and sizes. Programs should be tailored to meet organizational needs. However, a series of base measures must be used throughout any improvement effort. The IEEE Standards 1045, *Standard for Software Productivity Metrics* [1], and 982.1, *Standard Dictionary of Measures to Produce Reli-*

able Software [2], provide a starting point for defining the base measures. Using an external standard may be useful, because it allows comparison across multiple organizations and reduces the time required to deploy a measurement program.

The measures discussed in this section form the basis of a software measurement program. These measures are grouped in six categories:

- Size
- Defects
- Effort
- Duration
- Cost
- Customer satisfaction

4.3.1 Size

To measure our software processes, we need a measure of the size of the process deliverable. This provides us the capability to investigate measures such as organizational productivity or software quality. For instance, common measures of productivity are in terms of lines of code per day or function points per day. Quality is often cited in terms of defects per 1000 lines of source code (KSLOC) or defects per function point.

In determining "size," we need a measure that is standardized across projects and independent of the methodology, technology, or development tools used to create the software. Commonly cited measures of size include pages of documentation, number of objects, lines of code, or function points. Lines of code are typically measured without counting embedded comments in the source code and without special purpose code used only for testing and debugging. The SEI guidelines [3] for measuring lines of code is one standard that can be used to ensure that consistent definitions are used within the organization. Function points are a dimensionless number that is representative of the extent of the functionality of the software, hence, a size measure. Guidelines for counting function points are provided in publications available from the International Function Points User Group (IFPUG). Function points also enable consistent size definitions within an organization, independent of the programming language used for any project.

4.3.2 Defects

Organizations need to categorize and quantify defects in software processes. This enables the organization to develop measures of product quality, essential for determining how well the processes are working for the organization. Each organization needs to define defects clearly for its own processes. IEEE Standard 1044, *Software Quality Measures* [4], defines a framework for measuring defects.

4.3.3 Effort

The amount of work effort involved in developing and supporting software needs to be measured. Collecting these measures is helpful for estimation of project cost and staffing. Effort is typically measured in man-hours, man-months or man-years. The tracking effort is always related to a process or a part of a process. For example, we can track effort by life cycle phase or task.

4.3.4 Duration

One of the key measures is the calendar time required to complete a project, phase, or task. Collecting these measures and maintaining them in a database are helpful for assisting in estimation of project schedules. This time is usually expressed as elapsed time in days, and may initially be calculated as comparing the difference between the start date and the finish date. Later, duration may take into account such things as vacations, nonworked days, etc., to reflect the true elapsed time between a project's start and finish dates. Duration is tied to effort and may be correlated to other measures, such as software size.

4.3.5 Cost

Organizations need to measure the overall costs of developing and supporting software processes. Collecting these measures and maintaining them in a database are helpful for assisting in estimation of project cost. Each organization must have a clear definition of what will be included in this measure. The two major cost drivers in software development organization are the human and computer resource utilization. Cost is tied to effort and may be correlated to other measures, such as software size.

4.3.6 Customer Satisfaction

Software organizations need to focus on the needs of their customers. By measuring what is important to customers (for example, response time to process a query), software organizations can target specific areas of their processes for improvement.

4.4 EFFECTIVENESS OF PROCESS MEASUREMENT PROGRAMS

In this section, we will describe the attributes of an effective process measurement program and highlight positive and negative impact factors.

4.4.1 Attributes

The effectiveness of a software measurement program is not contingent on the existence of all of the attributes included in this section. However, a software process measurement program that lacks many of these attributes has a high risk of failure. The attributes were determined by combining experience gained by the authors and the writings of general management consultants, such as Deming and Juran, as well as software process improvement specialists like Watts Humphrey, who was the Director of the Software Process Program at the SEI. These attributes are:

Measurement is viewed as mission critical. Measurement is seen as a mission-critical function. The program is not seen as overhead, and it does not require continuous justification.

The measurement program is aligned with business objectives. The program is aligned with business objectives and helps in the determination of how well the business objectives are being met. The value and benefits of measurement are understood by clients and other corporate departments.

The measurement program is supported by management. Support for the program by all levels of management is demonstrated in the following ways:

- An empowered champion or sponsor leads the implementation and long-term support of the measurement program
- Staff who are responsible for the development and support

of the measurement program are selected based on their qualifications, not by their availability

- The importance of the program in the organization is demonstrated by the proactive participation of senior level personnel
- Management uses the measurement information to plan, control, and improve the processes and products of the organization
- The focus is on quantifiable process improvement, not on measurement

Measurement is linked to decision making. Appropriate measurement information is distributed to and used by all levels of management, as well as by team members. Measurement information is used to manage and estimate. Measurement information is used as part of the decision-making process with customers.

Action plans are derived from reported measurements. There are action plans for process improvement derived from measurement. Measurement provides evidence of the existence and magnitude of process improvements. This includes cost savings, increased quality, improved productivity, etc.

The measurement program is integrated into the development effort. The measurement program is integrated into the software development and support processes. This means the measurement tasks are included as part of the standard software development process. Where possible, software tools are acquired and incorporated into the development, test, and/or maintenance environments to facilitate the process of collecting the raw data. Raw data is collected, to the maximum extent possible, as a byproduct of the developer's (or maintainer's) daily activities, without requiring any added effort on their part.

The measures are standardized and documented. Accurate, repeatable, consistent data is maintained across all reporting entities (for example, effort tracking and size tracking). Consistent definitions of the measures are used across the organization to facilitate uniform understanding of the data. A loss or a change in personnel does not affect the quality and validity of data. Adherence to standards is audited. Continuous process improvement and the use of measurement data are included in an ongoing education program.

The program uses a balanced set of metrics. A balanced set of related metrics is used to gain a global and complete perspective. There is no reliance on a single metric for decision making. There is an appreciation of the value of several compatible metrics. The inherent risk to decision making from reliance on a single metric is recognized, and no single metric is viewed as a panacea.

The program is integrated with organizational initiatives. The measurement program is integrated with initiatives such as continuous process improvement or total quality management.

The program is part of the culture. Measurement is part of the corporate culture. Continuous improvement is demonstrated through measurement. The program remains sound despite turnover of personnel (at all levels), and it evolves to reflect changes in the business.

Measurement focuses on processes—not people. Measurement information is used to improve software processes, not to measure individual performance. The program measures the process, not the people.* It supports continuous process improvement.

4.4.2 Impact Factors

There are a number of factors that have been found by organizations to influence the effectiveness of their measurement programs. Some have a positive impact, and others have a negative one.

4.4.2.1 Positive Impact Factors

Organizations have found that some factors, when properly applied, exert a positive impact on their measurement programs. The factors are grouped according to:

- Business value
- Awareness
- Training

---

* Productivity may sometimes be mistakenly thought of as a people measure; however, productivity is really measuring the process in terms of its capability (in terms such as lines of code per day or some such similar measure) *across the organization*, not with respect to one individual developer. We look at process improvement with respect to its ability to improve productivity across the board for the entire organization, not individuals.

4.4.2.1.1 Business Value The factors related to business value include:

- Integrating the use of metrics into all levels of management decision making
- Demonstrating to line management the business value of measurement by providing management information
- Defining objectives for the measurement program
- Ensuring the appropriate use and presentation of the data (measure processes, not people)
- Communicating results promptly and appropriately
- Establishing realistic management expectations for measurement

4.4.2.1.2 Awareness The factors related to awareness include:

- Establishing strong public and private sponsorship at all levels, including high-level, committed corporate sponsorship
- Maintaining an awareness of the time required to conduct and implement measurement

4.4.2.1.3 Training The factors related to training include:

- Developing the measurement program with the same staffing consideration and disciplines as any other highly visible, high-risk project (phased approach, adequate resources, objectives, realistic time lines, etc.)
- Communicating the purpose, benefits, and vision for measurement to all levels of the organization, including all levels of management
- Including training and education on function points (if used by the organization), metrics, and data analysis for all measurement participants

4.4.2.2 Negative Impact Factors

The major factors that, when improperly applied, organizations have found to negatively impact their measurement programs fall in the categories of management and communication.

4.4.2.2.1 Management Factors related to management include:

- Lack of ongoing commitment or support from management (for example, underfunded, inadequately and inappropriately staffed, or lack of accountability)
- A view of measurement as a finite project
- Unclear goals and objectives for measurement
- Misuse of measurement data for individual performance reviews

4.4.2.2.2 Communication Factors related to communication include:

- Lack of communication of results and measurement information to the organization
- Negligence in responding to questions and concerns from staff about measurement
- Unmanaged expectations (for example, unrealistic time frames for implementing a measurement program)
- An expectation that measurement will automatically cause change

4.5 MEASUREMENT PROGRAMS IMPLEMENTATION STEPS

A measurement program does not magically appear. It must be implemented in stages. Table 4.1 lists phases and activities for implementing a measurement program. This is a suggested implementation. Each activity in the table is explained on the following pages.

This "project-based" approach to establishing a software measurement program ensures that appropriate up front planning is done before measurement begins. However, the exact order of the activities may vary from company to company. For example, some organizations need to establish sponsorship before defining goals. Once the "project" of implementing a measurement program is completed, the measurement program should be actively used to support management decision making. The most important steps in establishing a measurement program are to define the goals and objectives.

Table 4.1 Measurement Program Implementation

Section	Phase	Activities
4.5.1	Plan/evaluate	Definition of goals, objectives, and benefits
		Establishment of sponsorship
		Communication and promotion of measurement
		Identification of roles and responsibilites
4.5.2	Analyze	Audience analysis & target metrics identification
		Definition of software measures
		Definition of the data collection, analysis, and data storage approach
4.5.3	Implement/measure	Education
		Reporting and publishing results
4.5.4	Improve	Managing expectations
		Managing with metrics

It is critical that the defined goals of your measurement program directly apply to your organization's goals. This is the basis for determining what you will measure, what metrics you will use, and what data you need to collect based on the capabilities and maturity of your organization. The key is to look at the strategic and tactical goals of your organization and determine what you need to measure to provide management with information to track their progress towards their goals.

4.5.1 Plan/Evaluate Phase

4.5.1.1 Reasons for Implementation

One reason for measurement program failure is because the organization has a poor understanding of why they even began a measurement program. Measurement is viewed as a panacea, and measurement is performed for measurement's sake—not because they serve some specific purpose. A successful program must begin with a clear statement of purpose. The following list identifies some of the possible reasons for implementing a software measurement program in your organization:

- Establish a baseline from which to determine trends
- Quantify *how much* was delivered in terms the client understands
- Help in estimating and planning projects
- Compare the effectiveness and efficiency of current processes, tools, and techniques
- Identify and proliferate best practices
- Identify and implement changes that will result in productivity, quality, and cost improvements
- Establish an ongoing program for continuous improvement
- Quantitatively prove the success of improvement initiatives
- Establish better communication with customers
- Manage budgets for software development more effectively

4.5.1.2 Questions to Help Identify Goals

A measurement program will help in determining if the organization's goals are being met. To help determine if the strategic and tactical goals of your organization are being met, questions such as the following may need to be asked:

- How fast can we deliver reliable software to our customers? Does it satisfy their requirements?
- Can we efficiently estimate the development cost and schedule? Are the estimates accurate?
- What can we do to improve our systems-development life cycle and shorten the cycle time?
- What is the quality of the software we deliver? Has it improved with the introduction of new tools or techniques?
- How much are we spending to support existing software? Why does one system cost more than another to support?
- Which systems should be re-engineered or replaced? When?
- Should we buy or build new software systems?
- Are we becoming more effective and efficient at software development? Why? Why not?
- How can we better leverage our information technology?
- Has our investment in a particular technology increased our productivity?
- Where are our funds being expended?

If you cannot answer (with hard facts) the questions that your organization is asking, your organization needs a software measurement program.

The key selling point for a software measurement program is to provide a direct link between measurement data and the achievement of management goals. All levels of management need to understand how the data will provide them with facts that will help them manage and reach strategic and tactical goals. It is very important to obtain sponsorship and buy-in for your measurement program from managers in your organization who can financially commit to ensure its ongoing support and funding. You can establish buy-in by answering *What is in it for me?* for the entire organization.

4.5.1.3 Identification of Sponsors

An important step is to identify appropriate sponsors for the program. Because frequent initial reactions to software measurement include apprehension and fear, upper management support is key. Consider including upper and middle managers, project leaders, and clients as sponsors.

Sponsorship has to be won. Usually it takes time to establish solid sponsorship. You can start with limited sponsorship and then build on it as the program progresses. To receive continual support and to expand that support throughout your organization, you must sell the software measurement program to others. The following list includes some tactics that have been used to help establish buy-in for measurement:

- Provide education for the sponsors on measurement programs, software metrics, and methods to effectively implement change
- Use testimonials and experts to build credibility
- Identify issues in software development and maintenance, and show how a measurement program can help
- Address concerns directly and realistically. The following concerns may be addressed:
    How much resource time will it take to implement measurement?
    How much will it cost?
    Will individuals be measured?

Can we automate this process? (Automated counting, reporting, etc.)
How can we maintain consistency?
Where can we get help?
How long will it be before we will see results?
What is in it for me?
How will measurement benefit me?

Even with all of the prerequisites in place (clear sustainable objectives for measuring, phased-in plan, audience analysis), your measurement program will face a number of obstacles before becoming a part of your organization.

Several approaches can be used to sell software measurement to the rest of the organization:

- Present the program as an integral component to quality and productivity improvement efforts. Demonstrate that the measurement program allows you to:
  Track the changes in quality or performance, or both, resulting from improvements
  Identify improvement opportunities
- Present the benefits of the metrics program to each level of staff, describing in their own terms what is in it for them. These levels may include the professional staff, project managers, and senior management.
- Spread the word about measurement benefits as often and through as many channels as possible. There must be visible and demonstrable benefits, not just hype or industry claims. (For example, informal measurement discussions can occur around a coffee station.)
- Monitor the use of the data to ensure that it is used appropriately.
- Provide testimonials and concrete examples of measurement in practice, both within and outside of your organization. Note that internal successes and testimonials from respected colleagues are often worth much more than external examples
- Provide ongoing presentations at all levels.
- Address current user concerns. For example, if users are complaining about the amount of money spent on mainte-

nance, show comparisons of various applications normalized by application size.

- Address concerns and rumors about measurement candidly.
  Measurement fears (often from systems developers and analysts) are best dispelled by honestly addressing why measurement is needed and what benefits (for example, better
  estimates) will accrue from its use.
- Depersonalize measurement (that is, present data at a
  higher level of aggregation).

4.5.1.4 Identification of Roles and Responsibilities

When you establish a software measurement program, the roles and
responsibilities of participating individuals need to be defined and
communicated. The following questions need to be answered for your
organization:

- Who will decide what, how, and when to collect the measure-
  ment information?
- Who will be responsible for collecting the measurement in-
  formation?
- How will the data be collected? What standards (internal or
  external) will be used?
- At which phases will the data be collected? Where will it be
  stored?
- Who will ensure consistency of data reporting and collec-
  tion?
- Who will input and maintain the measurement informa-
  tion?
- Who will report measurement results? When?
- What will be reported to each level of management?
- Who will interpret and apply the measurement results?
- Who is responsible for training?
- Who will maintain an active interest in the measurement
  program to ensure full use of the measurement information?
- Who will evaluate measurement results and improve the
  measurement program?
- Who will ensure adequate funding support?

Generally, organizations with a software measurement program
have established a central measurement coordinator or coordina-

tors. For example, where an organization has established a Software Engineering Process Group (SEPG), some of these functions would be accomplished by it. Other functions may be performed by SQA. Still others may be performed by the software engineering organization. No matter how it is organized, the following responsibilities need to be enumerated and assigned.

- Review measurements for accuracy, completeness, and consistency
- Provide function point counting and other measurement assistance as necessary, if the organization uses function points as the basis for size estimation
- Distribute and support software measurement reporting
- Consult with management on the analysis, interpretation and application of the measurement information
- Maintain measurement data
- Collect and maintain attribute information for measurement analysis
- Maintain internal counting standards, requirements, and documentation for all collected measures
- Facilitate communication across the organization regarding the measurement program
- Establish and maintain software measurement standards and processes
- Provide education, training, and mentoring on all aspects of software measurement

Depending on the size and scope of your measurement program, the responsibilities listed below need to be assigned to individuals in your organization (as applicable).

- Schedule and coordinate the software measurements for development and/or enhancement projects
- Track all support changes for support reviews to keep baseline of measurements current
- Submit measurement information to the coordinator
- Schedule new applications to be counted after implementation
- Ensure adherence to measurement policies, measurement standards, and requirements

- Analyze, interpret, and apply resulting measurement information to improve development and support performance

4.5.2 Analysis Phase

*4.5.2.1 Analysis of Audience and Identification
of Target Metrics*

Once objectives have been set and sponsorship established, one of the next steps is to conduct an audience analysis and identify the target metrics. This activity should be conducted in conjunction with identifying roles and responsibilities discussed in the previous section. Work done here impacts the answers to the questions listed in the roles and responsibilities section.

Conduct an audience analysis so that you will be sure to measure and track the appropriate data that will help your organization reach its goals. The first step is to determine which groups of people will require and use the measurement data (for example, project managers, the CIO, and directors). Anticipate needs to identify concerns and objectives, and work with management to recommend a relevant set of metrics.

In applying these steps you should:

- Select the most important requirements that will meet the goals of your measurement program
- Set priorities and requirements for each audience
- Select only a few metrics to implement initially
- Select realistic and measurable metrics by starting small and then building on success
- Align audience needs with the overall objectives of measurement

In identifying metrics you should not:

- Choose metrics first and then create needs
- Try to satisfy all audiences and all requirements at once

4.5.2.2 Definition of Software Metrics

After you have conducted an audience analysis and identified your initial set of metrics, you need to clearly define all the measures that will make up the metrics. Identifying your metrics and defining your measures are important keys to assuring your data are collected consistently. You may wish to start from an existing set of standards. Enforcing the definitions and standards is just as important for maintaining consistency.

You need to define all the component measures that will make up the metrics so that the reason they were captured, their meaning, and their usage can be clearly communicated to measurement participants and management. If your measures are not clearly defined and understood by all individuals in your organization, your measurement data could be collected inconsistently and lose its reliability and usefulness

For example, if your goal is to determine whether development productivity is improving, you need to collect data on development hours, project type, and project size. If you do not specifically define what is included in development hours, some developers may report overtime hours while others may not. Some may include analysis hours before beginning the project while others may not. It is obvious that if the hours are not captured consistently, the productivity rate (a metric combining work effort and size) will not be valid. Furthermore, if you do not also specifically identify the type of project for which the data was collected, for example, command and control application vs. information system, you may wind up comparing apples to oranges. Some applications are more complex by their nature and require more hours of development time, given a specific application size in terms of lines of code.

There are many different approaches from which you may choose when first starting a software measurement program. Possible options include:

- Establishing a baseline of all applications in your organization as a function of application domain
- Running a measurement pilot project for one application
- Measuring activity against all installed applications
- Tracking only development projects
- Tracking defects, cost, and customer satisfaction
- Tracking only size and effort

The approach you select should be based on your own organizational goals and constraints for implementing a measurement program.

The following types of measures are often collected as part of an initial software measurement program:

- Lines of code
- Work effort
- Defects
- Cost
- Customer satisfaction

How you track and collect measurement data depends on what you decide to collect. If you choose to start big and collect a large amount of data for the whole organization, you might want to consider investing in automated data collection tools and repositories. In addition to the types of data, the data collection approach you choose will depend on the scope of the measurement program you want to establish. You need to establish your standards and processes for data collection, storage, and analysis to ensure that the data will be usable and consistently collected and reported.

Whether you build or buy automated measurement tools that will store and analyze your data depends on your requirements. Even if you start small and decide to store the information in a spreadsheet, you will quickly amass a large amount of data and will need to determine an electronic storage medium for collected data.

4.5.3   Implement/Measure Phase

4.5.3.1   Organizing for Just-in-Time Training and Education Processes

Education and training has to be provided to those persons who will be involved in and affected by the measurement program. Such an effort should be geared toward providing these individuals an understanding of:

- Why measurement is necessary
- How it affects them
- How the information can help them manage
- Their responsibilities in the context of the measurement program

Different types of training or presentations are required to address the needs of different levels of personnel, depending on the depth of their involvement. For example, managers may require an executive summary presentation on how measurement applies to them, while system experts may require in-depth training on data collection and measurement.

Particularly effective training incorporates realistic examples from the workplace of the participants. Complementary to formal training sessions, a follow up and support effort should be designed so that the participants "stay on course" and apply the skills they acquired during training. Monthly or quarterly follow up meetings where problems, success stories and difficulties in implementation are presented have also proved very effective.

When planning training and education programs one should always keep in mind that learning is enhanced by positive reinforcements and mostly FUN! Using graphical user interfaces in conjunction with good case studies and simulations has helped achieve these objectives.

4.5.3.2 Reporting and Publishing Results

Whether you produce manual reports, develop your own reporting system, or purchase a software measurement reporting package, you will need to report and publish the results. The following list includes suggested guidelines for publishing results:

- Make sure the people viewing the reports understand what the reports reveal so that the information is not misinterpreted and used to support poor decisions
- Include an analysis and explanation with the reported data (that is, mix graphs with text)
- Produce key statistics relevant to and usable by your audience
- Provide relevant and actionable reports to managers
- Use the appropriate graph to present your data (for example, pie charts do not present trends well)
- Keep graphs simple (that is, do not present multiple metrics on a single graph)
- Report source data in appendices

4.5.4 Improve Phase

4.5.4.1 Managing Expectations

If the life span of your projects ranges from a few months to a year or more, consider how long it will take to collect enough data points to make your data statistically significant. Also, it will take a great deal of time to define the measures, set the standards for data collection, and train the individuals. Since it will take a great deal of time before the measurement program will reach its long-term goals, one should also concentrate on short-term goals and let all involved know when they can expect to see more immediate results. The short term goals derive from the long-term goals. Keep your long-term goals in mind while developing short-term goals. For example, over the first few months of a new metrics program, improvement in estimating accuracy could be a more immediate goal than shortening the development cycle. Once you are able to collect work effort and project size, you can begin to supplement this data with available industry-data delivery rates to help you in project estimating and shortening the development cycle. The amount of time and money that must be invested in measurement before payback is realized varies from organization to organization. Many organizations have found that long-term payback may not be realized until two years or more after the program is implemented.

4.5.4.2 Managing with Metrics

The staff responsible for a metrics program is not usually responsible for making management decisions. A measurement program provides input to the decision-making process, but decision making is outside of measurement programs.

However, the most important process in a software measurement program is to use the results to support management decision making. This is the central purpose for a software measurement program, and it may be tied to continuous improvement, total quality management and other organizational initiatives. You can manage with metrics by:

- Analyzing attributes and data
- Incorporating results into decision-making
- Showing the cost-benefit

You need to analyze the attributes and determine which factors impact your processes. You also need to analyze the data to identify what is working and what is not, what areas require further investigation, and where opportunities for improvement exist

Incorporate the results and data into the management decision-making process in such areas as:

- Estimating time and cost of new development and enhancements
- Allocating resources to support and development areas
- Improving quality and productivity
- Analyzing portfolios
- Making the buy-versus-build decision

Using measures to manage is how you can show the cost-benefit of a measurement program. We conclude this chapter with five case study examples of measures describing demonstrating the benefits of measurement programs.

4.6   CASE STUDIES

A number of measures exist which can be utilized for managing the software development or maintenance effort. These give insight into the progress of the effort. This section includes five examples of such measures. Each of them, in and of themselves, do not necessarily tell a complete story, but if collected and utilized properly, provides effective warnings of potential problems.

4.6.1   Example 1: Staffing Profiles

Although this measure would appear on the surface to be one that is normally tracked, far too many organizations do not. We have found that many organizations fail to utilize some of the most basic and obvious measures necessary for effective program management.

Staffing profiles are one class of measure that would indicate if there are potentials for overruns or underruns. It is simply a profile of the planned staffing vs. the actual staffing (Figure 4.2). In this example, the actual staffing is lagging the planned staffing. This would indicate the potential for a schedule slip, since the staffing levels are below that which was estimated as necessary to accom-

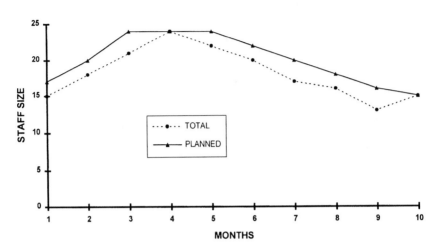

Figure 4.2 Planned vs. actual staffing.

plish the project's objectives. Whether this was actually occurring is not known, on the basis of this chart alone, but it would indicate that an investigation was necessary into what was occurring. Other data would be needed, such as a milestone chart, to see if progress was being maintained. Nonetheless, the chart served its purpose: to alert the project leader of a potential problem.

Clearly, if the staffing profile indicated that actual staffing exceeded the planned level, this could indicate the possibility of an overrun. As before, other data would be needed to confirm or reject the hypothesis. But as before, the chart would have served its purpose: to warn the project leader of a potential problem.

If supplemental information is added to these charts, expanded usage of these charts can be made for program management purposes. For instance, if we overlay onto these charts monthly data on staffing changes, i.e., additions to and losses of personnel on the project, it is possible to focus in more closely on the reasons for staffing shortfalls. If the changes to staffing are not negligible, the reasons for the shortfall may be due to a high turnover rate. This may be an indication of other problems, such as employee dissatisfaction. If the changes to staffing are negligible, the reasons for the shortfall may be a failure in obtaining the right personnel to meet the skill requirements. If we additionally overlay onto these charts monthly data on staffing levels by skill area or technical discipline (e.g., analysts, testers, quality assurance, etc.), it is possible to identify shortfalls in the technical disciplines necessary to implement the project's requirements.

4.6.2 Example 2: Software Size

As indicated earlier, software size is a measure essential for estimates of schedule, cost, and resources required to the accomplishment of a project's objectives.

If a software development organization estimates the size of the software to be produced, either in terms of lines of code or function points, stores that data in a database, and then tracks the project against these estimates (see Figure 4.3), it has the basis for performing rudimentary estimates of project schedule, cost, and required staffing. New startup projects can be compared against other projects in the database for similarity, and the schedule, cost, and staffing estimates can be made on the basis of what the similar project experienced. Clearly more accurate estimates can be made if the growth in size was also tracked, along with the related changes to schedule, cost, and staffing. Refinements and improvements in the ability to estimate can be accomplished if supplemental information is tracked, such as the number of requirements to be implemented by the project.

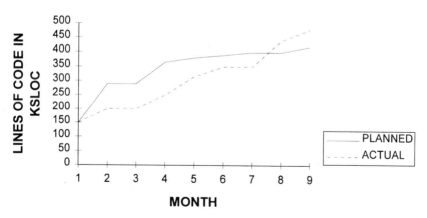

Figure 4.3 Software size.

Tracking software size can also provide indications of development problems. If the software size grows during the term of the project, there has to be a reason for it. It may be merely poor ability to estimate (most developers usually underestimate, often by as much as a factor of two or three). This can be resolved by recording and tracking estimates, as described in the paragraph above. Often, however, there may be other causes. For example, perhaps the requirements are changing. If the requirements are changing in a controlled fashion, and the impact of these changes are evaluated in terms of cost and schedule prior to accepting the changes, then there is no problem. On the other hand, if the size is changing due to uncontrolled requirements changes, then there is cause for concern. This can lead to schedule slips, cost overruns, and customer unhappiness. Perhaps the change in size is due to poor understanding of the requirements by the developers. Corrective action may be required, such as additional staff, staffing changes to acquire the necessary skills, or training for the existing staff in the necessary skills. Clearly additional data would have to be collected to zero in on the cause of the problem. But again, the measure served its purpose: to alert the project leader of a potential problem.

4.6.3   Example 3: Problem Report Tracking

Problem report tracking provides the capability to gain insight into both product quality and the ability of the organization to maintain the software.

Figure 4.4 plots, by week, the total number of problem reports, those still open, and those that have been closed. At the start of a new test phase, such as software integration testing, or acceptance testing, the number of problem reports opened would increase fairly rapidly, opening a gap between the number of problems reported and closed. If the problems are straightforward, we would expect the gap to decrease in short order. If not, that would be an indication of a possible problem.

Again, additional data is needed to zero in on the problem. The difficulty may not be a difficulty at all. It may be that the problems reported are of little operational consequence, and as a result, the resolution of them are being deferred to a later date. That would suggest that to make more effective use of this chart, it would be advisable to define categories of problem severity, and to overlay on

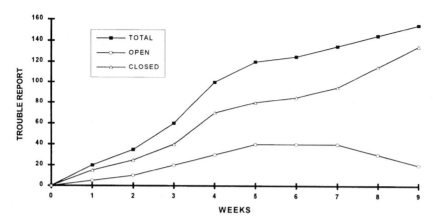

Figure 4.4 Problem report tracking.

this chart the number of problems open by severity category. On the other hand, a problem may be indicated, as described in the next paragraph.

To help in problem isolation, an additional set of charts that would be useful are bar charts of the number of weeks problem reports have been open at each severity level. For example, at the highest severity level, it would show the number open for one week, two weeks, three weeks, etc. If there are substantial numbers open for a long time, this could be an indication that the software is difficult to maintain, or that the staff that does not understand as well as it should the technical problem to be solved or corrected. Further investigation would be needed.

"Substantial numbers" and "open for a long time" are qualitative terms. There are no pat answers as to what is substantial or long. This is based on your organization's own experience and the complexity of the software under discussion. This suggests that it is advisable to maintain records from past projects for use for comparison.

4.6.4 Example 4: Control Charts of Newly Opened Bugs (by week)

Measures collected in real life environments often exhibit statistical variation. Such variation poses significant challenges to decision makers who attempt to filter out "signal" from "noise." By signal we mean events with significant effects on the data such as short or long term trends and patterns or one time, sporadic spikes. We do expect the number of newly reported bugs to fluctuate.

It is in the context of such fluctuation that we want to determine if the number of opened bugs, in a certain day, exceeds the "normal" range of fluctuation. Another phenomenon we are interested in identifying is a significantly decreasing trend in the number of opened bugs. Such a trend might be a prerequisite for a version release decision.

A primary tool for tracking data over time, in order to identify significant trends and sporadic spikes is the control chart. Control charts have been applied to industrial processes since the 1920s, first at Western Electric then expanding to U.S. industry, to Europe and, with outstanding results since the 1950s, in Japan. Control charts are the basic tools in process improvement and Statistical Process Control (SPC). Industrial Statisticians developed several types of control charts designed to handle a variety of situations. These charts can be applied to individual data points such as the number of bugs opened, per week, to representative samples, such as complexity of randomly selected modules, or to percentages, such as percent of line with comments. Sometimes data is collected simultaneously in several dimensions such as response times to a routine transaction at several stations in a network. Such multivariate (as opposed to univariate data) can be analyzed with multivariate control charts. A comprehensive discussion of control charts is beyond the scope of this book. We will focus here on interpreting real life examples. The interested reader can find more information on control chart in the univariate and multivariate case in books such as Kenett and Zacks [5] and Fuchs and Kenett [6].

All control charts consist of a graph tracking the relevant data and three lines: an Upper Control Limit (UCL), a central line and a Lower Control Limit (LCL).

Basic interpretation of control charts consists of monitoring the occurrence of three patterns:

1. A point below the Lower Control Limit or above the Upper Control Limit
2. A run of six points below or above the mean central line
3. A trend of six consecutive points going up or down

Any one of these events indicates a non-random occurrence that justifies appropriate action. As mentioned earlier downward trends in number of reported problems might trigger a version release, a point above the UCL might start an investigation as to the cause of this unusually high number of problem reports.

Figure 4.5 consists of an individual (I) and a moving range (MR) control chart for the number of new bugs per week reported in a beta test of a new software product from a company developing Rapid Application Development tools.

The I chart at the top tracks the number of new bugs. Superimposed on this chart are three lines:

- The Upper Control Limit (UCL = 68.99) located three standard deviations above the mean number of new bugs
- The mean number of new bugs (MU = 38.24) computed as the total number of reported new bugs divided by the number of observation weeks
- The Lower Control Limit (LCL = 7.484) located three standard deviations below the mean number of new bugs

The MR chart at the bottom tracks successive differences in the number of new bugs. The MR chart tracks variation in number of

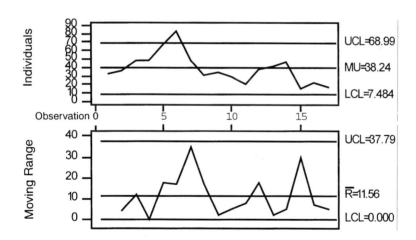

Figure 4.5 Control chart for number of newly opened bugs (by week).

reported new bugs and is used to compute the standard deviation used in the I chart. Superimposed on this chart are also three lines:

- The Upper Control Limit (UCL = 37.79) for the moving ranges
- The average moving range (MU = 11.56)
- The Lower Control Limit (LCL = 70) for the moving ranges

Analyzing the lower MR chart shows no unusual, non-random, patterns. The I chart however indicates a significant increase in the number of reported bugs on week 6 and a short run of three weeks below average toward the end. If this pattern is sustained for three more weeks management could declare that the number of reported new bugs has significantly dropped, thus allowing for version release. Overall the average number of new bugs has been 38.2 per week.

4.6.5 Example 5: Control Charts of Closed Bugs (by week)

In this example the number of closed bugs, per week is tracked on an I and MR control chart (Figure 4.6). Analyzing the lower MR chart shows a period were the number of closed bugs per week remained almost constant (week 8–14) thus producing very low moving ranges (successive differences being almost zero). The I chart

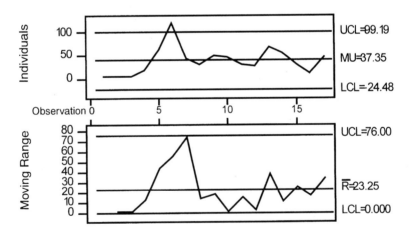

Figure 4.6 Control chart for number of closed bugs (by week).

indicates a significant increase in the number of closed bugs on week six indicating a quick response to the significant increase in number of reported bugs identified above. Overall the average number of bugs closed per week has been 37.3, just a bit lower than the number of reported new bugs per week.

4.7 SUMMARY

This chapter provided an introduction to software measurement programs. After elaborating on the question *Why Measure?*, and key definitions, the Goal-Question-Metric method is presented followed by a section on the effectiveness of process measurement programs. In that section attributes of an effective program are listed together with positive and negative impact factors. A four-step implementation plan is discussed in detail so that practitioners can tailor this program to their own organization-specific needs. Finally we conclude with five case studies that provide real life examples of how measures are used in software development and maintenance organizations.

REFERENCES

1. ANSI/IEEE Standard 1045. *Standard for Software Productivity Metrics*, IEEE Standards Office, Piscataway, NJ.
2. ANSI/IEEE Standard 982.1. *Standard Dictionary of Measures to Produce Reliable Software*, IEEE Standards Office, Piscataway, NJ.
3. CMU/SEI-92-TR-20. *Software Size Measurement: A Framework for Counting Source Statements*.
4. IEEE Standard 1044. *Software Quality Measures*, IEEE Standards Office, Piscataway, NJ.
5. Kenett, R.S. and Zacks, S. *Modern Industrial Statistics: Design and Control of Quality and Reliability*, Duxbury Press, 1998.
6. Fuchs, C. and Kenett, R.S. *Multivariate Quality Control: Theory and Applications*, Marcel Dekker Inc., 1998.

5
Quality of Software Products and Documents

5.1. INTRODUCTION

In the previous chapter, we spoke of the development and implementation of measurement programs that can be used for determining the current level of performance of the processes used to develop software. Measures can also be used to evaluate the efficacy of process improvement efforts. In other words, we can use these measures to see how well our current processes are performing and for determining if proposed changes to the process will improve the overall level of performance.

Measures of product quality are integral to the determination of process quality. For instance, measures of product quality, such as fault density (which we will discuss in this chapter), define the current capability of the process. We can determine the nominal value and the three-sigma Upper Control Limit of fault density across all projects, say, at the end of the coding and unit testing phase. This characterizes the current status of the process. We can pilot a change in the process for this phase of activity and measure the nominal value and the three-sigma Upper Control Limit of fault density achieved on the pilot project. We can use this as one determinant of whether or not to make a permanent change in the process.

In this chapter, we will describe a number of measures of product quality that can be utilized in measurement programs, thus enabling us to characterize the current state of the process, and providing a benchmark to evaluate the impact of process changes.

5.1.1 Dimensions of Product Quality

Product quality has many dimensions. Software product quality has been classified into Functionality, Usability, Reliability, Performance and Serviceability (FURPS). Hewlett-Packard pioneered this quality model in the late 1970s. It has now been adopted by many organizations and integrated into an international standard ISO/ IEC 9126 [1]. We begin by defining these terms.

Functionality: The product has necessary function to accomplish the user's task.

Usability: The product is easy to use in terms of accomplishing its desired task. It is easy to learn. The user can interact effectively with the product to enhance productivity. Effective training and documentation is available.

Reliability: This relates to the frequency and severity of program errors and recovery attributes. How much can the user rely on the program results?

Performance: This relates to efficiency, i.e., the speed with which the product executes its functions. Included are overall throughput, memory utilization, and response time.

Serviceability: This relates to technical support, response time and quality of corrections; easiness of installation procedures.

The FURPS dimensions provide a broad classification of software product quality. The ISO 9126 standard elaborates on the FURPS classification and maps these broad characteristics into subcharacteristics as follows:

Characteristic	Subcharacteristic
Functionality	Suitability
	Accuracy
	Interoperability
	Security
Reliability	Maturity
	Fault tolerance
	Recoverability
Usability	Understandability
	Learnability
	Operability
Efficiency	Time behavior
	Resource behavior

Maintainability	Analyzability
	Changeability
	Stability
	Testability
Portability	Adaptability
	Instability
	Conformance
	Replaceability

Kitchenhan and Pfleeger [9] discuss this and other related models pointing out the generality of the ISO 9126 model and the fact that it cannot be tested. The FURPS and ISO 9126 models should therefore be considered only as abstract non-measurable constructs.

In this chapter we will elaborate on these dimensions in order to achieve detailed and focused information on software product quality characteristics. For example, we provide an operational definition of specification document accuracy. Such definitions are critical to our ability to control and improve the various aspects of product quality. Keeping this in mind, quality models such as FURPS and ISO 9126 can only serve qualitatively as a checks and balance mechanism. They help us make sure that we don't look for the key under the lamppost, and that we measure what needs to be measured.

5.1.2 Assessing Product Quality

Assessments of product quality determines the ability of the software or corresponding documentation (e.g., specifications, design descriptions) to meet user's needs. If the quality is poor, users/customers are unhappy. Furthermore, those assigned to maintain the software will also be unhappy, since the burden of correcting the software and cleaning up the documentation will fall on their shoulders. Often, no attempt is made to clean up the documentation, and the maintainers effectively fly by the seats of their pants when it comes to identifying and isolating the cause of the failure, and correcting the software.

There are a number of measures that can be applied for assessing product quality. These include measures such as problem report

trends, problem report aging, defect density, and failure interval. These have been classified as product quality measures by the
Joint Group on Systems Engineering [2]. IEEE Standard 982.1 [4]
identifies additional measures as product quality measures. These
include, among others, the better known measures, such as fault
density, defect density, cyclomatic complexity, requirements traceability, and software maturity index. Both references provide good
detail on how to calculate these measures. We will describe only a
few of these measures and refer the reader to the cited documents
for a more detailed discussion of them.

5.1.2.1 Problem Report Tracking

Problem report trends and problem report aging quantify the total
number of problem reports written, those still open, those that have
been closed, and the length of time problem reports have remained
open. These are also identified by severity of the reported problems.
These measures have been described in Section 4.6.3 under problem
report tracking. They are considered product quality indicators inso-
far as they are an indicator of the amount of rework required. High
quality software requires minimal rework.

5.1.2.2 Defect Density

Defect density assesses product quality by normalizing the number
of defects detected in the software by the software size. Defects are
effectively synonymous with faults (see Chapter 6 for definitions of
errors, faults, and failures). Typical metrics are defects per thousand
lines of source code (KSLOC) or per function points. Depending on
how the data are collected, this measure can be used to identify
which components of the software have the most quality-related
problems, or to establish quality levels for the software product at
various points in the development cycle.

Defect density accumulates the numbers of defects detected as
a result of design or code inspections conducted during specific
phases of development effort. The basic measure is:

$$DD = \sum_{i=1}^{I} D_i / KSLOD \text{ (or KSLOC)},$$

where

D_i = Total number of unique defects detected during ith design or code inspection
I = Total number of inspections during that phase,
KSLOD = Total number of lines of design statements, in thousands (for design inspections)
KSLOC = Total number of source lines of executable code or nonexecutable data statements, in thousands (for code inspections, or where estimates of the lines of code are available on the basis of expansion from the known lines of design statements)

The basis for evaluation is comparison against experience on past projects. There are no absolute values for this measure or industry standards to compare against.

Figure 5.1 illustrates the defect density measure. In the example, the notation "PDR" and "CDR" refer to formal reviews. The PDR or Preliminary Design Review is a review that is sometimes held after the architectural design of the software is essentially completed to serve as a quality gate for the beginning of the detailed design of the individual units of code. The CDR or Critical Design Review, is usually held after the detailed design is substantially com-

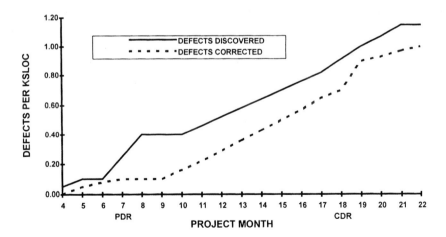

Figure 5.1   Defect density example.

pleted. It can be inferred from this chart that some detailed design began before the PDR was completed, and was completed after the CDR. This is not necessarily unusual. On the other hand, it could be an indicator of a problem if the CDR was held too early, i.e., before enough of the detailed design was completed to get a handle on the overall adequacy of the design.

The use of formal reviews is sometimes incorrectly viewed as imposing a waterfall development model. Formal reviews can be held at points in the development process where a significant portion of an activity, such as detailed design, has been substantially completed. If conducted properly, a formal review can be a very effective means of "looking at the forest, instead of the trees." While reviews that are microscopic in nature, such as a unit-level peer review, are essential, it is also necessary to step back and assume a view across the product to ensure that all the pieces fit together.

Note that the defects corrected are also overlaid on the chart, thus providing additional useful information.

5.1.2.3   Fault Density

Fault density is a measure that is similar to defect density. Whereas the defect density measure tends to provide an indicator of the quality of the evolving software during design, fault density is a quality indicator used during the testing activities. It can also be used during operational usage of the software.

Again, the basis for evaluation is comparison against experience on past projects. Here, too, there are no absolute values for this measure or industry standards to compare against.

Figure 5.2 illustrates the fault density measure. In this example (although not shown on the chart), the testing activities covered software integration. Note that some early coding of the software was implemented. Also note that the integration of the software has not been completed on schedule, since there are still some open problem reports. Rework and retest will be required. The advantage of overlaying the "faults corrected" data is that additional insight into quality and program management issues can be obtained.

5.1.2.4   Cyclomatic Complexity

This measure is used as an indicator of the potential for low reliability of the software, as well as the ability to maintain the software.

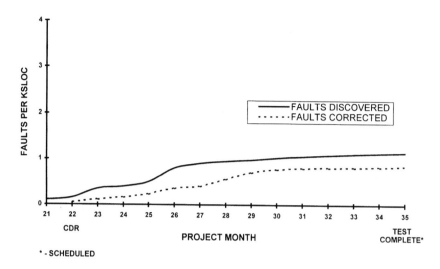

Figure 5.2 Fault density.

A number of studies have indicated correlation of the value of the complexity measure with the probability of defects [3]. The theory is that the higher the cyclomatic complexity, the greater the potential was for the developer to have introduced errors, thus lowering the quality of the software. Furthermore, the higher the complexity, the lower the understandability of the software, thus making it more difficult for a maintainer to follow the logic and isolate problems. It can be calculated for single units of code or aggregates of units of code.

The basic equation is:

$$C = E - N + 1$$

where
    N = Number of nodes (sequential groups of program statements
    E = Number of edges (program flows between nodes)

Cyclomatic complexity can be calculated from either structured design language statements or from source code statements. A usual limit for cyclomatic complexity is 10. It is often set lower for avionics software, where a limit of 7 may sometimes be set. Such limits are often stated in the organization's design and coding standards.

These limits are not to be exceeded in the code, as delivered, nor after any rework.

A number of tools exist which can read both the structured design language statements and the source code. This permits evaluations of the complexity to begin early on in the development effort, continuing on through coding and test.

5.1.2.5 Requirements Traceability

A number of requirements traceability tools exist which facilitate the tracking of requirements from the highest level specification down to the individual line of code. These tools simplify the process of keeping track of where the requirements have been implemented, and facilitate the analysis of the impact of changes. However, in addition to this, there is a simple measure that can be applied that quantifies the degree of traceability achieved. The measure is:

$$TM = (R1/R2)*100$$

where

TM = Traceability
$R1$ = Number of requirements implemented in the phase of the effort under investigation
$R2$ = Total number of requirements applicable to the phase of the effort.

Clearly, by the end of any phase of the software development effort, the value should be very close to 100%. Unimplemented requirements will mean that the software will not perform as intended.

5.1.2.6 Software Maturity Index

The software maturity index is an indicator of the stability of the software product. It is based on the number of changes that occur for each release of a product. It is calculated from the following formula:

$$SMI = [M_T - (F_a + F_c + F_d)]/M_T$$

where

M_T = The number of modules in the current release
F_c = The number of modules in the current release that have been changed

TRACKING CHANGES IN A 1,000 MODULE APPLICATION

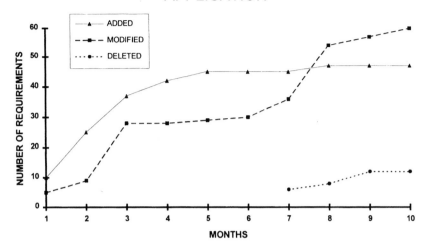

Figure 5.3 Software maturity index.

F_a = The number of modules in the current release that have been added

F_d = The number of modules from the previous release that were deleted in the current release.

The product is considered more stable as the value of SMI approaches 1.0. In the example in Figure 5.3, we see that in the ten months since the last release of a 1000 module application, 47 modules were added, 60 were modified, and 12 were deleted. Consequently, SMI is calculated to be 0.881. It is starting to stabilize. Even from inspection of the figure, it can be seen that the number of added and deleted modules appear to be leveling off, while the number of modified modules continues to rise.

5.2 SOFTWARE SPECIFICATIONS METRICS

In the previous section, we described a sampling of measures that can be used as indicators of software product quality. These measures were primarily oriented toward evaluations of the code or design representations of the code. In this section, we will look at measures of the quality of documentation used to describe the requirements and design of the code.

5.2.1 Introduction to Software Specifications Metrics

Following the development of system requirements, the software specification document forms a first definition of the software product. Each of the following phases of design, coding, and integration/testing transforms the initial software specifications into lower levels of machine implementable details until the final machine-processable object code is generated. Therefore, the quality and completeness of the software specification directly influences the quality of the final software product.

The purpose of software specification metrics is to provide quantitative measures of the quality of the software specification document. These metrics are designed to complement good "engineering judgment" that is required to judge the quality of the software specification documents. Quantitative measures can reveal characteristics of quality. These metrics are established by coupling documentation structure with systematic engineering methodology to measure documentation completeness, consistency, and other characteristics of document quality.

The quality of a software specification document is defined to be determined by how well the interface, performance, and quality assurance requirements satisfy the following measures:

- Completeness
- Accuracy
- Correctness
- Consistency
- Readability
- Testability

Of the above six measures of document quality, the specification metrics discussed in this section addresses the following three measures: completeness; accuracy; and readability. For each of these quality measures, a set of metric formulas will be established. These formulas are based on pioneering work done in the early 1980s at Logicon and on metrics listed in IEEE 982.1 [4]. These formulas characterize the quality of the software specification document. When the values from groups of formulas are examined, then a collective evaluation of each of the three measures (i.e., completeness, accuracy, and readability) can be quantitatively measured.

These specification metrics do not provide a comprehensive evaluation of document quality. Qualitative engineering judgments is still required in each measure. The measure of "completeness" is one of the primary focuses of the specification metrics since its characteristics are most amenable to quantitative measures. The measures of "correctness" and "testability" do not have any specification metrics identified. Evaluations of these measures require qualitative engineering judgment.

5.2.2 Overview of the Specification Metrics Methodology

The specification metrics methodology is a series of analysis steps to systematically evaluate and quantify the quality of the program document (see Figure 5.4). Upon receipt of the software specification document, the program performance and interface requirements are parsed into requirements categories. During this parsing, the data is evaluated to determine whether the data is ambiguous, missing, or inconsistent.

The second step processes the parsed data using statistical analysis in order to derive the specification metrics. These formulas provide quantitative values which can be compared against an eval-

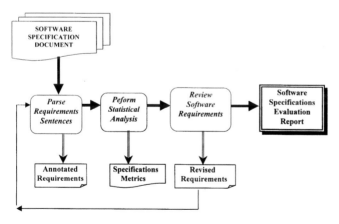

Figure 5.4 Specification metrics methodology.

uation scale to determine the degree of compliance with accepted measures of program specification quality. The specification metrics are evaluated for each function within the specification document to identify specific deficiencies as well as point to trends of deficiency and/or areas of complexity requiring further clarification.

By combining the evaluation for all functions within the program specification document, a determination of overall program specification quality can be assessed. The specific numeric value derived from this process can be compared against limits of benchmark measures of quality derived from historical data. Since specific numeric values are calculated in the evaluation, it is easy to determine the areas requiring correction in the specification document.

5.2.3 Parsing Requirements/Attribute Definitions

The first two steps in applying the specification metrics methodology are to identify requirement sentences and then parse these sentences into attributes of specification sentences.

The attributes of a sentence are:

1. Initiator of action
2. Conditions for action
3. Action
4. Constraints on action
5. Object of action
6. Immediate source of object
7. Immediate destination of object
8. Mechanization of action
9. Reason for action

Identification of specification sentences is discussed in Section 5.2.3.1, and the semantic rules which define attributes are discussed in Section 5.2.3.2.

5.2.3.1 *Identifying Specification Sentences*

A specification or requirement sentence contains information that defines what operations a system, subsystem, or function are to perform and under what constraints these operations occur. Normally, these sentences contain the verb "shall," which differentiate them from purely commentary or descriptive sentences. The following paragraphs discuss instances in which sentences do not correspond exactly with English sentences.

The parsing preceding the computation of software specification metrics requires minimal perturbation of the original sentence structure when decomposing a sentence into its attributes. There exist conditions where sentences must be defined in other than the strict English context.

One such condition is when compound sentences are encountered, connected by "and" or a semicolon. These sentences are split into two (or more) sentences for evaluation purposes.

Another example of sentence rewriting occurs when the sentence is written in the passive voice, usually indicated by presence of the verb "be." In these cases the sentence is rewritten into active voice and an implied initiator is inserted if necessary. For example,

" An RSI shall be provided when either of the following conditions occur . . . "
would be rewritten (for analysis purposes only) as:

"[Remote Status Reporting] shall provide an RSI when either of the following conditions occur . . ."

When an implied subject is needed, such as in the above example, it is always taken to be the title of the immediate function which contains the sentence.

Specifications parsing operates on sentences, and thus tables and figures present problems. Figures are assumed to be clarification of verbal information within the text—as such, figures are not directly analyzed. Tables may contain stand-alone information, and hence their information is restructured into sentences. In particular, I/O tables are rewritten as one requirement sentence per I/O item, as shown next.

5.2.3.1.1 Referencing Sentence. Function 1—Inputs: The inputs shall be as described in the following specification table.

Type	Source	Units	Limits	Accuracy	Frequency
Activity initiation request	application software	N/A	N/A	N/A	On request
Elapsed time indicator	Timer control	N/A	N/A	N/A	On request

5.2.3.1.2 Parsed Translated Specification Sentence.

Specification Sample 1: Function 1 shall input the activity Initiation Request from the application software on request.

Specification Sample 2: Function 1 shall input the elapsed time indicator from the timer control on request.

5.2.3.2 Attribute Definitions

The following nine sub-sections present full definitions for the nine sentence attributes listed at the beginning of Section 5.2.3. We conclude this sub-section with examples of parsing for four typical sample sentences (see Figure 5.5).

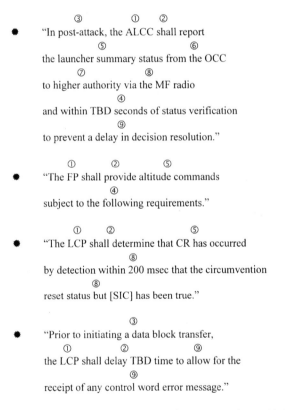

Figure 5.5 Sample parsing of sentences into attributes.

5.2.3.2.1 Initiator of Action. Initiator of Action is the subsystem, function or subfunction which causes the action. Initiators may be applied, as is frequently true when the action is passive but are required attributes in all sentences. The initiator is analogous to the subject in English grammar.

5.2.3.2.2 Action. There are two types of action: positive and negative. A positive action is the information processing or transfer of data as performed by the Initiator. A negative action is the assignment of constraints to an operation. Examples of positive actions are shown in the first three sample sentences; the last sample sentence shows a negative action. Action is analogous to the main verb in English grammar, and is a required attribute for all sentences.

5.2.3.2.3 Conditions For Action. The Conditions for Actions are the prerequisite states, activities, and/or data which are necessary for the action to occur. Examples include frequency of invocation, necessary completion of some preliminary processing sequence, and necessary processing state before entry into some operation. Conditions for actions are not a required attribute for all sentences.

5.2.3.2.4 Constraints on Action. The Constraints on Action define the boundary conditions enforced on the action after initiation. Constraints bound influence, define termination criteria, and specify limits. Examples of constraints include numerical tolerances and time durations. Constraints on actions are not a required attribute for all sentences.

5.2.3.2.5 Object of Action. The Object of Action is the subsystem, function, subfunction, or data item which is being acted on by initiator via the action The object of the action is not a required attribute for all sentences.

5.2.3.2.6 Source of Object. The Source of Object is the immediate subsystem, function, subfunction, or information structure (data base) from which the object originates. Source is applicable only if the object is an item of information which is being transferred by the Initiator, such as in the first sample sentence.

5.2.3.2.7 Destination of Object. The Destination of Object is the immediate subsystem, function, subfunction, or information structure (data base) where the object is sent. Destination is applicable only if the object is an item of information which is being transferred by the initiator, such as in the first sample sentence.

5.2.3.2.8   Mechanization of Action. Mechanization of Action answers the question: "How is the action accomplished?" Mechanization levies implementation-specific constraints, such as shown in the third example, where CR must be determined by checking the circumvention reset status bit. Mechanization is never a required attribute.

5.2.3.2.9   Reason for Action. Reason for Action provides the rationale for the action. This information is not strictly necessary, but often helps to clarify the intent of a requirement sentence. The first and last sample sentences contain Reason attributes.

5.2.4   Specification Metrics Definition

The quality of a software specification document is determined by how well the interface, performance, and quality assurance requirements satisfy measures of completeness, accuracy, and readability. These measures applied to a software specification document are used to produce the Software Specification Evaluation Report.

The function is the basic entity of the specification document. It specifies a feature of the software system which should match a customer requirement. A function corresponds to one or more sentences in the specification document. In some cases functions are described in a table format and need to be parsed into equivalent sentences.

After parsing we can compute, for each function, the following measures:

N1   Total number of sentences

N2   Total number of attributes in sentences of corresponding function

N3   Total number of missing attributes in sentences of corresponding function

N4   Total number of ambiguous attributes in sentences of corresponding function

N5   Total number of missing source attributes in sentences of corresponding function

N6   Total number of missing destination attributes in sentences of corresponding function

N7   Total number of ambiguous source attributes in sentences of corresponding function

N8   Total number of ambiguous destination attributes in sentences of corresponding function

N9   Total number of source attributes in sentences of corresponding function

N10   Total number of destination attributes in sentences of corresponding function

N11   Total number of technically valid attributes in sentences of corresponding function

N12   Total number of TBD in sentences of corresponding function

N13   Total number of missing conditions attributes in sentences of corresponding function

N14   Total number of missing constraints in sentences of corresponding function

N15   Total number of descriptive sentences in sentences of corresponding function

From these measures we compute, for each function, the following metrics:

SM1   Missing information = Total number of missing attributes/Total number of attributes = $N3/N2$

SM2   Ambiguous information = Total number of ambiguous attributes/Total number of attributes = $N4/N2$

SM3   Functional connectivity = (Missing or ambiguous source attributes + missing or ambiguous destination attributes)/Total number of source and destination attributes = $(N5 + N6 + N7 + N8)/(N9 + N10)$

SM4   Attributes presence = Total number of valid attributes = $N11$

SM5   TBD frequency = Total number of TBD/Total number of attributes = $N12/N2$

SM6   Missing condition information = Total number of missing condition attributes/Total number of sentences = $N13/N1$

SM7   Missing constraints information = Total number of missing constraints/Total number of sentences = $N14/N1$

SM8   Descriptive information = Total number of descriptive sentences/Total number of sentences = $N15/N1$

5.2.5 Metric Evaluation Criteria

Each metric is evaluated and assigned one of four possible classifications. The four classifications are blue, green, yellow, and red.

Blue   Exceeds all required performance levels
Green   Complies with required performance levels
Yellow Contains some deficiencies in performance levels
Red   Contains major deficiencies in performance levels

Blue and green are considered acceptable, yellow and red are considered unacceptable.

If any single specification metric is calculated as being in the red zone, both the function and the evaluation category is labeled red.

Each organization has to determine its color boundaries. This is usually done by analyzing past data. The following table provides sample values that delineate the four color classifications, per function.

For example values of SM1 between 0 and 1/200 qualify as "Blue." Values between 1/200 and 2.5/200 qualify as "Green," values between 2.5/200 and 5/200 as "Yellow." Anything beyond 5/200 is considered "Red." We deliberately set the classification limits as ratios to facilitate their interpretation. For example over five missing attributes per 200 attributes qualifies as "Red."

	Blue	Green	Yellow	Red
I. Completeness				
SM1—Missing information	0	1/200	2.5/200	5/200
SM2—Ambiguous information	0	1/200	2.5/200	5/200
SM3—Functional connectivity	0	1/200	2.5/200	5/200
SM4—Attribute presence	9	6	4	3.5
SM5—Fault TBD presence	0	1/200	1/20	1/2
II. Readability				
SM3—Functional connectivity	0	1/200	2.5/200	5/200
SM8—Descriptive information	1/3	1/6	1/9	1/19
III. Accuracy				
SM2—Ambiguous information	0	1/200	2.5/200	5/200
SM5—Fault TBD presence	0	1/200	1/20	1/2
SM6—Missing condition information	0	1/200	1/100	1/50
SM7—Missing constraints information	0	1/200	1/100	1/50

In order to combine the metric values in a given category, the values must be normalized to the same scale such as a 0 to 1 scale. The normalization factors and resulting normalized scales are provided in the following table. The normalized metrics can now be summed directly and form an evaluation scale for each of completeness, readability, and accuracy. These scales are summed to produce the function summary scale.

	Blue	Green	Yellow	Red
I. Completeness				
Missing information—SM1*40	0	.2	.5	1
Ambiguous information—SM2*40	0	.2	.5	1
Functional connectivity—SM3*40	0	.2	.5	1
Attribute presence—(9-SM4)/5.5	0	.54	.9	1
Fault TBD presence—SM5*2	0	.01	.1	1
Total	0	1.15	2.5	5
II. Readability				
Functional connectivity—SM3*40	0	.2	.5	1
Descriptive information—(.33-SM8)/.28	0	.65	.87	1
Total	0	.85	1.37	2
III. Accuracy				
Ambiguous information—SM2*40	0	.2	.5	1
Fault TBD presence—SM5*2	0	.01	.1	1
Missing condition information—SM6*50	0	.25	.5	1
Missing constraints information—SM7*50	0	.25	.5	1
Total	0	.71	2.5	4

The next two tables show a full example with five functions and all three metric categories. Every category value for each function can be assigned a color according to prespecified weighted category scales. Such weights can be determined through formal or informal risk analysis. The function summaries are determined by summing the category values for each function. The category summaries are calculated by summing the weighted function values.

Systems are defined as a collection of functions sometimes organized in subsystems. The system summary totals are calculated by aggregating values over all functions. The number of functions is used as a multiplier to calibrate the color scales. For example if subsystem X has three functions, than subsystem summary values above 33 are determined red.

Category	Weight	Blue	Green	Yellow	Red
Total weighted completeness (Wc)	34%	0	1.15	2.5	5
Total weighted readability (Wr)	33%	0	.85	1.37	2
Total weighted accuracy (Wa)	33%	0	0.7	2.5	4
Function summary:		0	2.7	6.37	11

By normalizing the specification metrics we can evaluate directly, for each function, the weighted characteristics. Function Completeness, Readability and Accuracy are derived by simply adding the normalized metrics

- Function completeness $= 40 * (SM1 + SM2 + SM3)$
  $+ (9 - SM4)/5.5 + 2 * SM5$
- Function readability $= 40 * SM3 + (.33 - SM8)/.25$
- Function accuracy $= 40 * SM2 + 2 * SM5$
  $+ 50 * SM6 + 50 * SM7$

and then, using the weights we determined for Completeness, Readability and Accuracy, we compute the function summary as:

$$\text{Function Summary} = Wc\{\text{Function Completeness}\}$$
$$+ Wr\{\text{Function Readability}\}$$
$$+ Wa\{\text{Function Accuracy}\}$$
$$= Wc\{40 * (SM1 + SM2 + SM3)$$
$$+ (9 - SM4)/5.5 + 2 * SM5\}$$
$$+ Wr\{40 * SM3 + (.33 - SM8)/.25\}$$
$$+ Wa\{40 * SM2 + 2 * SM5$$
$$+ 50 * SM6 + 50 * SM7\}$$

Similar computations can be derived for systems that consist of several functions. Overall system categories are calculated as:

- System Completeness $= \Sigma$ function completeness over all subsystems
- System Readability $= \Sigma$ function readability over all subsystems
- System Accuracy $= \Sigma$ function accuracy over all subsystems

and then compute the overall system summary as:

$$\text{System Summary} = \text{Wc\{system completeness\}}$$
$$+ \text{Wr\{system readability\}}$$
$$+ \text{Wa\{system accuracy\}}$$

Software System Specification Evaluation Report—Quantitative Format

		Categories			
Subsystem	Weight	Completeness 34%	Readability 33%	Accuracy 33%	System Summary
Subsys. #1	15%	6.6	1.2	1.5	3.1
Subsys. #2	23%	11.3	10.5	11.6	11.1
Subsys. #3	32%	38.4	12.8	18.2	23.1
Subsys. #4	15%	1.0	5.1	2.1	2.7
Subsys. #5	15%	29.7	28.6	59.1	39.1
Category Summ.		20.5	11.8	17.9	16.7

Software System Specification Evaluation Report—Qualitative Format

		Categories			
Subsystem	Weight	Completeness 34%	Readability 33%	Accuracy 33%	System Summary
Subsys. #1	15%	Blue	Blue	Blue	Blue
Subsys. #2	23%	Green	Green	Green	Green
Subsys. #3	32%	Yellow	Green	Yellow	Yellow
Subsys. #4	15%	Blue	Blue	Blue	Blue
Subsys. #5	15%	Yellow	Red	Red	Red
Category Sum.		Yellow	Red	Red	Red

5.3 DOCUMENTATION READABILITY METRICS

5.3.1 Readability of Software Documentation and Technical Manuals

Technical manuals and software documentation are often written in such a way that the users of the manuals cannot understand them. Since the 1920s many people have studied the problem of determining whether a text sample is readable or not. One way to make text easier to understand is to write it at an appropriate reading grade level for its intended audience.

A phrase is a sequence of words, centered on a core element called the head, that constitutes a coherent grammatical unit of the same basic type as the head. A clause is a larger unit, one that resembles a simple sentence in its parts and their arrangement. In traditional terms the major units in a clause are a subject and a predicate. The subject is some type of noun or noun phrase, but the predicate may have as its central unit a verb, an adjective, a noun phrase, a prepositional phrase, or an adverb. A clause may be viewed as specifying a relation among various participants, each identified by a noun phrase and playing a certain role in the clause.

A sentence with only one clause is said to be simple; a sentence with more than one clause is complex. Short sentences made up of short words are easier to understand than long sentences made up of long words (Flesch, 1974 [5]). It has become standard practice for companies to specify writing guidelines (e.g. GM, Digital [6,7]). In the next section we present various metrics that were developed to determine the readability level of a document.

5.3.2   Readability Metric

5.3.2.1   The Flesch Reading Grade Level Metric

Flesch's reading index requires counting sentences, words and syllables in the text samples. The grade level indicates the number of years of education of an average English-speaking reader that can understand the measured text.

Let

TSEN = Total number of sentences in the text sample
TWORD = Total number of words in the sample
TSYL = Total number of syllables in the sampleet

The average number of words in a sentence (AWORD) and average number of syllables in a word (ASYL) are computed as:

AWORD = AWORD/TSEN
ASYL = TSYL/TWORD

Standard writing averages approximately 17 words per sentence and 147 syllables per 100 words.

The Flesch Reading Grade Level (GL) is computed using the following formula:

$$GL = 0.39*AWORD + 11.8*ASYL-15.59$$

Round off the GL value to the nearest tenth. A Reading Grade Level of 7–8 is considered standard. Values of 4–5 are considered easy and 15–16 very difficult.

5.3.2.2 The Kincaid Overall Grade Level Metric

The Department of Defense document Mil-M-38784A: "Manuals, Technical: General Style and Format Requirements" [8], specifies a formula developed by J. Kincaid for measuring readability of military technical manuals by military personnel. The procuring activity uses this metric to determine compliance. The Kincaid Overall Grade Level Metric is calculated using a specified number of 200-word samples that depends on the size of the manual in pages. The Flesch Reading Grade Level is determined for each sample. The average grade level has to be within one unit of the required reading grade level, however some samples can have grade levels up to 3 units above the required level. This approach allows for relatively complicated sections to be written at a somewhat higher reading level than the rest of the manual.

5.3.2.3 The Passive Sentences Metric

In order to compute this metric sentences have to be first classified as active or passive. The passive sentences metric is the percentage of passive sentences:

Passive Sentence Metric = (Number of active sentences)/(total number of sentences)

Writing experts commonly advise to avoid passive sentences unless the person or thing performing the action is unimportant.

The Passive Sentences Metric, the Flesch and the Kincaid reading indices do not address issues of information accessibility and overall document design. Moreover linguists attribute the meaning of words not only to the text itself but also to the context of the text such as cultural factors, local and personal interpretations and definitions. Language engineering is a developing technology concerned with the improvement of verbal and written communication. Such improvements are necessary if one wants to avoid mishaps due to inconsistency in procedures or simple misunderstandings, especially in multinational organizations.

5.4 SUMMARY

This chapter focused on measuring and assessing the quality of software products and related documents. The first section described the dimensions of product quality first in an abstract, conceptual framework and then on a precisely quantifiable basis. A special section elaborates on assessing the quality of software specification documents. Such documents are critical to the success of the software development effort. Moreover, identifying omissions and problems in specification documents is considerably more cost effective than relying on testing of the final product for preventing customers from experiencing failures. Specification errors are more efficiently corrected BEFORE any transformation of the problematic requirement into the system occurs. Alternatively the error has to be identified through testing, then skillful (and expensive) analysts have to be employed to identify the fault causing the failure. For this reason we should invest substantially in identifying error-prone areas in specification documents. The last two sections in this chapter were focused on metrics that are used to assess specification documents.

REFERENCES

1. ISO/IEC Standard 9126. *Information Technology—Software Product Evaluation–Quality Characteristics and Guidelines for Their Use*, International Organization for Standardization, Geneva, 1992.
2. Joint Logistics Commanders Joint Group on Systems Engineering. *Practical Software Measurement: A Guide to Objective Program Insight*, Version 2.1, 1996.
3. Pressman, Roger S. *Software Engineering: A Practitioner's Approach*, 2nd ed., New York: McGraw-Hill Book Company, 1987.
4. ANSI/IEEE Standard 982.1. *Standard Dictionary of Measures to Produce Reliable Software*, IEEE Standards Office, Piscataway, NJ.

5. Flesch, R. *The Art of Readable Writing*, Harper and Row, New York, 1974.

6. General Motors. *S.T.A.R. General Motors Computerized Simple Test Approach for Readability, A Tool for Improved Communication*, Public Relation Staff, General Motors Corporation, Detroit, 1973.

7. Digital Equipment Corporation. *Personal Computer Documentor's Guide*, 1983.

8. Mil-M-38784A. *Manuals, Technical: General Format and Style Requirements*, Amendment 5, 1978, 1983.

9. Kitchenham, B. and Pfleeger, S. "Software Quality: The Elusive Target," IEEE Software, Vol. 12, No. 1, (1996), pp. 12–21.

6
Software Reliability Control

6.1 INTRODUCTION

This chapter discusses methods to asses software reliability through dynamic tests so that it can be controlled and improved. In particular, we will show how to determine software reliability from data collected in various forms and stages of testing. We begin with an introduction to software testing and proceed with fundamental definitions and concepts of software reliability. Basic tools for the analysis of defect data are presented, followed by a more mathematical treatment of software reliability models. The chapter concludes with a section on software reliability estimation.

Varying amounts of time and money are commonly devoted to testing software before it is released to field use or shipped as a product. General approaches to software testing include:

- Functional Testing: tests of user functions of the software
- Coverage Testing: tests of various paths through the software
- Partition Testing: the software's input domain is divided according to homogeneous classes, and tests are performed for each class
- Statistical Testing: uses a formal experimental paradigm for random testing according to a usage model of the software

Good engineering practice recommends planning the testing effort in parallel to requirements analysis and high level design. Such plans are documented in a test plan document.

The Test Plan is typically defined at three levels: Unit Tests, Integration Tests, and System Tests. The objective is to cover, through actual testing, the functions defined in the product requirement and specification document and in the design description document. The test plan is compared to these documents in order to determine the level of coverage that it provides. The test plan document describes the function being tested, the test case itself, and the expected result. A report sheet, related to all cases provided in the test plan, is eventually completed by the tester. A typical test plan document consists of the following:

   a.   List of test cases
   b.   Test environment
   c.   Test cases classification
   d.   Prerequisite conditions for performing the tests
   e.   Expected test results

Unit Tests are written and performed after coding is completed by the software developer. It is referred to as "white box" testing. White box testing is design-based testing where, the basis for the testing is the detailed design of the unit (sometimes referred to as modules). A unit is considered ready only when the unit test report is completed. Areas covered by the Unit Tests include:

   a.   Basic functionality tests
   b.   Boundary and limitations tests
   c.   User interface validity tests
   d.   Environment and portability tests
   e.   Abnormal conditions tests

The testing itself is performed according to the test plan document. Test reports are issued by the tester indicating what worked and what went wrong.

Integration Testing is performed on a subsystem once all unit tests are completed. In this case, the basis for the testing is the design of interfaces between collections of units. Integration testing tests functionality of a group of units (modules) according to specified data interfaces and calling sequences. It includes functional testing and testing the behavior of related units in case of software and hardware failures. Memory and disk resource utilization checks are typically also performed. Some of the areas covered in integration tests include:

    a. Normal operations
    b. Abnormal operations
    c. Activating of module interface options
    d. Synchronization testing
    e. Error recovery from hardware and software errors
    f. Calling sequences
    g. Data integrity

System Testing is typically performed at the application level after integration testing has been completed. System testing tests the software application's functionality and performance for compliance with the requirements documented in the product requirements specification . It is referred to as "black box" testing in that the requirements (not the design) are the basis for structuring the test cases to be executed during system testing. Some of the areas covered in system tests include:

    a. Normal operations
    b. Abnormal operations
    c. Functionality and performance
    d. External interfaces
    e. Error recovery from hardware and software errors

In order to put into context these various forms of testing we present next a benchmark case study.

6.2 THE HITACHI SOFTWARE ENGINEERING CASE STUDY

The Japanese software industry has a long and distinguishes record of considering the quality of software they ship to their customers as a critical success factor. Hitachi Software Engineering Company, a part of Hitachi, is one of the largest software houses in Japan. About 20 percent of the systems developed at Hitachi Software have five million lines of code, while the average size of a system is about 200,000 lines of code. Hitachi Software uses statistical control to improve both the quality of the software they ship and the quality of the process they use to develop it. Onoma and Yamura [1] provide a glimpse at the software development methods developed over 20 years of trial and error at Hitachi Software.

    The software development life cycle at Hitachi is based on the basic loop of *developing*, *testing*, and *fixing* commonly known as the waterfall model. Hitachi specifies 10 steps as listed below:

1. Feasibility study
2. Project planning
3. Basic design and validation
4. Functional design
5. Structural design
6. Module design, coding and unit tests.
7. System test
8. Product verification
9. System simulation test
10. Product release

The development process is divided into three departments: design, quality assurance, and production administration. The design department develops software and carries responsibilities for cost and schedule, as well as the quality of requirements specification, design documentation, manuals and, ultimately, the product itself.

The quality assurance department has no responsibility for cost and scheduling, but carries full responsibility for product quality after release. The production administration department manages the production schedule.

	Design Department	Quality Assurance Department
Feasibility study		
	Project planning	**Product release**
	Basic design and validation	**System simulation**
	Functional design	**Product verification**
	Structural design	**System test**
	Module design, coding, and unit tests	

(1)-(2)-(3) ---- **(4)** ----- **(5)** ---- **(6)** ---- **(7)** ----- **(8)** ---- **(9)** ---- **(10)** ----- >

Hitachi software development life cycle

The process begins in the design department. After development, when the design department declares that the quality of the product is satisfactory and development work is at least 80% complete, the quality assurance department administers an initial *quality probe*. In a quality probe, testers in the quality assurance department run a small percentage of the functional test items. If the results are satisfactory, the product goes into product verification for more extensive testing. If the results of the quality probe are poor, the quality assurance department refuses to do any further testing and sends the product back to the design department for improvements. This loop is reiterated until the product passes in verification tests, after which it goes on to the final test, a system simulation test. At this stage the product is tested in a user environment simulation. When all tests are successfully completed, the quality assurance department authorizes shipment to the customer. The diagram on p. 158 is a schematic representation of the Hitachi software development life cycle.

Before debugging, programmers use requirements specifications to explicitly design and specify tests for unit and system debugging. Hitachi's procedures include the systematic application of Program Checking Lists (PCL) to be run during source code debugging. PCLs consist of a description of the input data, expected outputs, a priority classification indicating the relative importance of the test and an item classification. Hitachi uses four categories:

- Basic functional tests (60% of PCLs)
- Boundary conditions tests (10% of PCLs)
- Abnormal conditions tests (15% of PCLs)
- Portability and environment tests (15% of PCLs)

The general guidelines specify about one PCL per 10 to 15 lines of code. Batch programs are tested with fewer PCLs than on-line programs.

We will revisit the Hitachi case study later in the chapter.

6.3 DEFINITIONS OF SOFTWARE RELIABILITY

A necessary first step in any analysis of data is to establish definitions and terminology. Problems reported as a result of testing and regular usage by customers are recorded as Modification Requests (MRs), Trouble Reports (TRs), or Authorized Program Analysis Reports (APARs), or some similar designation. Such reports document a departure from user requirements and performance deficiencies. We call these events *failures*.

Developers can track the defect in the program that caused the failure. We call these defects *faults*. Another common term used to describe faults is "bugs."

An *error* is the root cause of software faults that can potentially lead to software failures. This potential is realized when a user or a user-simulation triggers, under given conditions, an input stimulus that reveals the software fault, thus creating a failure.

These definitions are based on the official terminology set in the IEEE Standard Glossary of Software Engineering Terminology [2] which specifies the following:

Error: "Human action that results in software containing a fault. Examples include omissions or misinterpretation of user requirements in a software specification, incorrect translation, or omission of a requirement in the design specification."

Fault: "(1) An accidental condition that causes a functional unit to fail to perform its required function (2) A manifestation of an error in software. A fault, if encountered, may cause a failure. Synonymous with a bug."

Failure: "(1) The termination of the ability of a functional unit to perform its required function (2) An event in which a system component does not perform a required function within specified limits. A failure may be produced when a fault is encountered."

Customer satisfaction is determined by experience with actual usage of the software. It is sometimes measured as *failures / 1000 CPU hours*.

Process quality is determined by errors introduced during the process. Development process quality is often measured by *faults / 1000 source lines*.

We will use the terms "error," "defect," or "anomaly" in a generic sense. The terms "fault" and "failure" will be reserved to have the technical definitions presented above.

The next section introduces the reader to software reliability models that are used in the analysis of software defects.

6.4　SOFTWARE RELIABILITY MODELS

The standard definition of software reliability is the probability of execution without failure for some specified interval, called the mission time. This definition is compatible with that used for hardware reliability, though the failure mechanisms may differ significantly. Software reliability is applicable both as a tool complementing development testing, in which faults are found and removed, and for certification testing, when a software product is either accepted or rejected. As early as in 1978, the now obsolete MIL-STD-1679(Navy) [3] document specified that one error per 70,000 machine instruction words, which degrades performance with a reasonable alternative work-around solution, is allowed; and one error causing inconvenience and annoyance is allowed for every 35,000 machine instruction words. However, no errors which causes a program to stop or degrade performance without alternative work-around solutions are allowed.

These reliability specifications should be verified with a specified level of confidence. Interpreting failure data is also used to determine if a product can be moved from development to beta testing with selected customers, and than from beta testing to official shipping. Both applications to development testing and certification testing rely on mathematical models for tracking and predicting software reliability. Many software reliability models have been suggested in the literature (for a review see Wood [4]). In this section, we cover four basic software reliability models.

6.4.1 The Jelinski and Moranda "De-Eutrophication" Model

Jelinski and Moranda, while working for the McDonnell Douglas Astronautics Company, published one of the first practical software reliability models [5]. They developed a model for use on a number of modules of the Apollo program. The model assumptions are:

a. The rate of error detection is proportional to the current error content of a program.
b. All errors are equally likely to occur and are independent of each other.
c. Each error is of the same order of severity as any other error.
d. The error rate remains constant over the interval between error occurrences.
e. The software is operated in a similar manner as the anticipated operational usage.
f. The errors are corrected instantaneously without introduction of new errors into the program.

Clearly it is difficult to envision a situation in which a perfect error correction process is achieved. However, the instantaneously corrected error part of the assumption can be avoided by not counting errors which were previously detected, but were not corrected. Assumption (c) can be avoided by dividing the errors into classes based upon severity. For instance, one might have a category for critical errors, a category for less serious errors, and one for minor errors. Separate software reliability models are then developed for each category.

Using assumptions (a), (b), (d), and (f), the failure rate is defined as:

$Z(t) = \phi [N - (i - 1)]$, where t is any time point between the discovery of the $(i - 1)$th error and the ith error. The quantity ϕ is the proportionality constant given in assumption (a). N is the total number of errors initially in the system. Hence, if $i - 1$ errors have been discovered by time t, there are $N - (i - 1)$ remaining errors so the hazard rate is proportional to this remaining number. Figure 6.1 is a plot of the hazard rate versus time. As can been seen, the rate is reduced by the same amount ϕ at the time of each error detection.

Let $X_i = t_i - t_{i-1}$, i.e., the time between the discovery of the ith and the $(i - 1)$st error for $i = 1, \ldots, n$ where $t_0 = 0$, using assumption (d), the X_i's are assumed to have an exponential distribution with rate $Z(t_i)$. That is:

$$f(X_i) = \phi[N - (i - 1)] \exp\{- \phi[N - (i - 1)] X_i\}$$

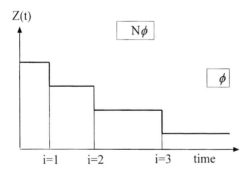

Figure 6.1 The de-eutrophication process.

The joint density of all the X_i, using assumption (b) is:

$$L(X_1, \ldots X_n) = \prod_{i=1}^{n} f(X_i)$$

$$= \prod_{i=1}^{n} \phi[N - (i - 1)]\exp\{-\phi[N - (i - 1)]X_i\}$$

Taking the partial derivatives of $L(\mathbf{X})$ with respect to N and ϕ and setting the resulting equations equal to zero, the solutions for the following set of equations are obtained as maximum likelihood estimators, $\hat{N}$ and $\hat{\phi}$, for N, and ϕ respectively.

$$\hat{\phi} = \frac{n}{\hat{N}\left(\sum_{i=1}^{n} X_i\right) - \sum_{i=1}^{n} (i - 1)X_i}$$

and

$$\sum_{i=1}^{n} \frac{1}{\hat{N} - (i - 1)} = \frac{n}{\hat{N} - \dfrac{1}{\displaystyle\sum_{i=1}^{n} X_i}\left(\sum_{i=1}^{n} (i - 1)X_i\right)}$$

which can be solved numerically using numerical techniques such as Newton-Raphson iterations. Once we computed $\hat{N}$ we derive $\hat{\phi}$ from the first equation.

The estimate of the MTTF (Mean Time To Failure) is derived, after the jth occurrence, as:

$$\text{Estimated MTTF after } j\text{th error} = \frac{1}{\hat{Z}(t_j)} = \frac{1}{\hat{\phi}(\hat{N} - j)}$$

The estimated time to remove the next m errors, after observing n failures, can be easily derived as:

Estimated time to remove the next m errors

$$= \sum_{j=n+1}^{n+m} \frac{1}{\hat{\phi}(\hat{N} - j + 1)}.$$

The data required for the calculations of these estimates is either the time between error occurrences, X_i , or the time of error occurrences, t_i, $i = 1, \ldots n$.

The biggest problem in seeking the estimates is the difficulty in convergence of the numerical techniques employed to find the maximum likelihood estimators. Difficulties include lack of convergence, sensitivity of the iteration scheme to the starting value, convergence to a saddle point or invalid estimate, and non-uniqueness of the estimates. Littlewood and Verall [6] have shown that a unique maximum at finite $\hat{N}$ and non-zero ϕ is attained if, and only if,

$$\frac{\displaystyle\sum_{i=1}^{n} (i - 1)X_i}{\displaystyle\sum_{i=1}^{n} (i - 1)} > \frac{\displaystyle\sum_{i=1}^{n} X_i}{n}$$

Otherwise there is no convergence and $\hat{N}$ is infinity. Essentially this condition means that the model can only be applied to software that exhibits software growth, i.e. $X_i > X_{i-1}$. In any computer implementation of this model, the previous condition should first be verified to ensure a unique finite maximum exists.

Jelinski and Moranda's model cannot be applied to software programs which are not complete. The program under test has to be relatively stable with a total number of N errors present initially in the code. Various extensions of this basic model have been proposed. These include an evolving program which accounts for the completion percentage, error rates proportional to program size, non-homogeneous distributions of errors, error rates proportional both to the number of errors remaining and to the time spent testing and models accounting for varying testing efforts and programmers ability (see Musa, Iannino, and Okumuto [7]).

We introduce in the next section with an extension of the Jelinski-Moranda model proposed by Lipow [8]. The extension allows for more than one error occurrence during a testing interval. This is well suited to situations were data is aggregated over time. Since failure data is usually reported on a weekly or monthly basis this extension proved very useful.

6.4.2 The Lipow Extension Model

The Lipow model assumes that:

   a. The rate of error detection is proportional to the current error content of a program
   b. All errors are equally likely to occur and are independent of each other
   c. Each error is of the same order of severity as any other error
   d. The error rate remains constant over the testing interval
   e. The software is operated in a similar manner as the anticipated operational usage
   f. During a testing interval i, f_i errors are discovered but only n_i errors are corrected in the time frame

Assumptions (a) to (e) are identical to the assumptions of the Jelinski-Moranda model. Assumption (f) is different. Suppose there are M periods of testing in which testing interval i is of length x_i. during this time frame, f_i errors are discovered, of which n_i are corrected. Assuming the error rate remains constant during each of the M testing periods (assumption (d)), the failure rate during the ith testing period is:

$$Z(t) = \phi[N - F_i], \qquad t_{i-1} \le t \le t_i$$

where ϕ is the proportionality constant, N is again the total number of errors initially present in the program, $F_{i-1} = \sum_{j=1}^{i-1} n_j$ is the total number of errors corrected up through the $(i - 1)$st testing intervals, and t_i is the time measured in either CPU or wall clock time at the end of the ith testing interval, $x_i = t_i - t_{i-1}$. The t_i's are fixed and thus, are not fixed as in the Jelinski-Moranda model. Taking the number of failures, f_i, in the *i*th interval to be a Poisson random variable with mean $Z(t_i)x_i$, the likelihood is:

$$L(f_1, \ldots f_M) = \prod_{i=1}^{M} \frac{[\phi[N - F_{i-1}]x_i]^{f_i} \exp\{-\phi[N - F_{i-1}]x_i\}}{f_i!}$$

Taking the partial derivatives of $L(\mathbf{f})$ with respect to ϕ and N and setting the resulting equations to zero, we derive the following equations satisfied by the maximum likelihood estimators $\hat{\phi}$ and $\hat{N}$ of ϕ and N:

$$\hat{\phi} = \frac{F_M/A}{\hat{N} + 1 - B/A} \qquad \text{and} \qquad \frac{F_M}{\hat{N} + 1 - B/A} = \sum_{i=1}^{M} \frac{f_i}{\hat{N} - F_{i-1}}.$$

where

$F_M = \sum_{i=1}^{M} f_i$, the total number of errors found in the M periods of testing, $B = \sum_{i=1}^{M} (F_{i-1} + 1)x_i$, and $A = \sum_{i=1}^{M} x_i$, the total length of the testing period.

From these estimates, the maximum likelihood estimate of the mean time until the next failure (MTTF) given the information accumulated in the M testing periods = $1/\hat{\phi}\ (\hat{N} - F_M)$.

6.4.3 A Case Study of the Lipow Model

In order to demonstrate the application of Lipow's extension to the Jelinski and Moranda De-Eutrophication model we will quote some data collected at Bell Laboratories during the development of the No. 5 Electronic Switching System.

The data consists of failures observed during four consecutive testing periods of equal length and intensity:

Test period	Observed failures	Predicted failures
1	72	74
2	70	67
3	57	60
4	50	54
5		49
6		44
7		40

The Lipow model produces the following estimates:

$\hat{N}$ = 762 and $\hat{\phi}$ = 0.097, i.e. an estimate of 762 for the initial number of failures and 0.097 for the proportionality constant representing the reduction in failure rate due to removing one fault from the system.

The column of predicted failures in test periods 5, 6, and 7 is computed from the Lipow model with the above estimates for ϕ and N. Comparing observed and predicted values over the first 4 test periods can help us evaluate how well the Lipow model fits the data.

The Chi-square goodness of fit test statistics is 0.63, indicating extremely good fit (at a significance level better than 0.001). We can therefore provide reliable predictions for the number of failures expected at test periods 5–7, provided the test effort continues at the same intensity and that test periods are of same length as before.

The Jelinski-Moranda model and the various extensions to this model are classified as time domain models. They rely on a physical modeling of the appearance and fixing of software failures. The different sets of assumptions are translated into differences in mathematical formulations (see Neufelder [9] and Musa et al. [7]). A model free approach, that does not require the analyst to specify a physical model, has been proposed by Kenett and Pollak in the 1986 issue of the IEEE transactions in Reliability. The Kenett-Pollak model exploits optimality properties of Bayesian procedures known as Shiryayev-Roberts procedures. The obvious advantage of this model is that it is assumption free and thus more robust in actual applications. However the mathematical complexity of the model being beyond the scope of this book we refer the interested reader for details on this approach to Kenett and Pollak [10,11] and Kenett and Zacks [13].

When software is in operation, failure rates can be computed by computing number of failures, say, per hours of operation. The predicted failure rate corresponding to the steady state behavior of the software is usually a key indicator of great interest. The predicted failure rate may be regarded as high when compared to other systems. We should keep in mind, however, that the specific weight of the failures indicating severity of impact is not accounted for within the failure category being tracked. In the bug tracking data base, all failures within one category are equal.

Actual micro-interpretation of the predicted failure rates, accounting for operational profile and specific failure impact, is therefore quite complex. Predicted failure rates should therefore be considered in management decisions at a macro, aggregated level. For instance, the decision to promote software from system test status to acceptance test status can be based on a comparison of predicted failure rates to actual.

Kanoun, Kaaniche, and Laprie [19] analyze four systems (telephony, defense, interface, and management) and derive average failure rates over 10 testing periods and predicted failure rates. Their results are presented below:

System	Predicted failure rate	Average failure rate over 10 test periods
Telephony	1.2×10^{-6}/hour	1.0×10^{-5}/hour
Defense	1.4×10^{-5}/hour	1.6×10^{-5}/hour
Interface	2.9×10^{-5}/hour	3.7×10^{-5}/hour
Management	8.5×10^{-6}/hour	2.0×10^{-5}/hour

As expected in reliability growth processes, in all systems, the average failure rate over 10 test periods is higher than the predicted failure rates. However, the differences in the defense and management systems are smaller indicating that these systems have almost reached steady state, and no significant reliability improvements should be expected. The telephony and interface systems, however, are still evolving. A decision to promote the defense and interface systems to acceptance test status is therefore supported by the data.

6.4.4 Pragmatic Software Reliability Estimation

A simple model for estimating software reliability has been proposed by Wall and Ferguson [12]. The model relies on the basic premise that the failure rate of software decreases as more software is used and tested. The relationship proposed for this phenomena is:

$$C1 = C0 \left(\frac{M1}{M0} \right)^{a}$$

where:

$C1$ = Future period cumulative number of errors

$C0$ = Previous period cumulative number of errors—a constant determined empirically

$M1$ = Units of test effort in future period (e.g. number of tests, testing weeks, CPU time)

$M0$ = test units in previous period—a scaleable constant

a = Growth index—a constant determined empirically by plotting the cumulative number of errors on a logarithmic scale or by using the following formula:

$$a = \frac{\log\left(\dfrac{C1}{C0}\right)}{\log\left(\dfrac{M1}{M0}\right)}$$

The failure rate, Z(t), is derived from the following formula:

$$Z(t) = \frac{dC1}{dt} = aC0 \frac{d\left(\dfrac{M1}{M0}\right)}{dt} \left(\frac{M1}{M0}\right)^{a-1}$$

This model is based on several assumptions:

a. Software test domain is stable i.e. no new features are introduced.
b. Software errors are independent.
c. Errors detected are corrected within the same test period.
d. Testing is incremental so that new tests are introduced in subsequent testing periods.

Revisiting the data used in the previous section, with an empirically derived estimate of 0.8 for a, we get an estimated number of failures for test period 5 of 47.17 failures. The Lipow model predicted 49 failures (see Figure 6.2).

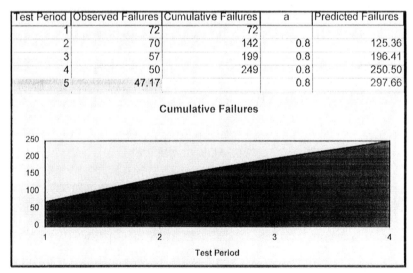

Test Period	Observed Failures	Cumulative Failures	a	Predicted Failures
1	72	72		
2	70	142	0.8	125.36
3	57	199	0.8	196.41
4	50	249	0.8	250.50
5	47.17		0.8	297.66

Figure 6.2 Pragmatic software reliability estimation.

6.4.5 Data Domain Models Using Statistically Designed Testing Experiments

Software testing or mission simulation consists of verifying software output under varying input conditions. Data domain models are based on the partitioning of the input space into subsets. Let **n** be the number of inputs in the sample which are chosen from the input space E at random, according to the probability distribution pi of input subsets. Let N_e be the number of inputs, out of **n** inputs, that causes failures. The probability of success $P = 1 - N_e/n$. Improving the probability of success, **P**, can be achieved by finding and correcting errors in the software program per each input condition. However, the challenge with this approach is detecting all the errors through the many possible input combinations.

Since we may never be able to test each combination, a method is required for identifying the input subsets used in the actual tests. By breaking the software functionality into specific operating zones, the software code can be exercised with combinations of inputs using boundary analysis to identify whether the software can handle the various zone inputs. Thus software testing would encompass the full range of functionality as opposed to the execution duration method.

Designing the data domain experiment involves three initial steps:

1. Identifying the software input test factors
2. Setting the factor levels
3. Determining the operating range zones such as nominal level, lower limit, upper limit, above upper limit, below lower limit

The number of all possible test combinations is cb^a where:

a = Number of factors
b = Number of factor levels
c = Number of operating range elements

As an example we will consider evaluating the reliability of software controlling the movement of an electronic microscope of an automatic testing system incorporating pattern recognition and electro-optical technologies. The system is used to test, on-line, micro-electronics devices as part of the production process in modern automated factories. The software was designed and implemented with Object Oriented methodologies.

The factors to be considered for testing include:

A. Electro-mechanical motor speed
B. Lighting conditions
C. Environment noise levels
D. Size of device under test
E. Shape of device under test

If we set two levels for each factor (high and low) and identify five operating range zone elements (nominal, upper limit, lower limit, above upper limit, below lower limit), the number of possible tests is: $5 \times (2)^5 = 160$.

Statistical methodology provides techniques for constructing experimental arrays that allow for efficient experimentation and testing. The experimental array that corresponds to the testing of all possible combinations of factors levels is labeled a Full Factorial Array. In our example such an array consists of 160 tests or experimental runs.

An alternative array is the Fractional Factorial Array which is a selected subset of all possible combinations. The following table provides an example of such a reduced experimental array with eight test points and $8 \times 5 = 40$ test runs. The symbols $-$ and $+$ stand for high and low levels of the corresponding factors labeled A to E. The symbols N, UL, LL, >UL, and <LL stand for nominal, upper limit, lower limit, above upper limit and below lower limit, respectively. Each test point is performed five times, under all operating zone elements. Successful tests are labeled S, failed tests are labeled F.

Test point	Test factors					Operating range zones				
	A	B	C	D	E	N	UL	LL	>UL	<LL
1	−	−	−	+	+	S	S	S	S	S
2	+	−	−	−	−	S	S	S	S	F
3	−	+	−	−	+	S	S	S	F	S
4	+	+	−	+	−	F	F	F	F	F
5	−	−	+	+	−	S	F	S	S	S
6	+	−	+	−	+	S	S	S	S	S
7	−	+	+	−	−	S	F	S	F	S
8	+	+	+	+	+	S	S	S	S	S

The 40 test runs produced 10 failures yielding a probability of success = 75%.

The effectiveness of the test program can be determined by the ratio of actual test runs to the total number of possible input combinations in a full experimental array. The above test program's effectiveness is therefore 40/160 = 25%. For more details on statistically designed experiments see chapters 11 and 12 in the book by Kenett and Zacks [13].

Partial applications of factorial and fractional factorial arrays have been proposed in the software and computer science literature (see, for example, Binder [21] and Tartalja and Milutinovic [20]). The application of statistical methodology to software testing remains, however, a largely unexplored domain.

Several authors proposed to derive estimates of software reliability by stratifying the input space into regions which can then be assigned weights that reflect user workload profiles.

If n_j runs are made in region j which carries weight W_j, and f_j failures are observed, the estimate of software reliability or probability of success becomes:

$$P = 1 - \sum_{j=1}^{K} \frac{f_j}{n_j} W_j$$

For more information on data software reliability estimation using domain models see Brown and Lipow [14] and Nelson [15].

6.5 SOFTWARE RELIABILITY ESTIMATION AND TRACKING

Software reliability estimation and tracking is an engineering management activity designed to:

- Determine the reliability of delivered software
- Evaluate the product at each milestone in the software life cycle
- Formalize data collection and maintenance of historical data

The basic steps in software reliability estimation and tracking are:

1. Identify the system to be studied, including associated systems and hardware configurations that will be involved in system testing.
2. Determine reliability goals and classify failures into severity classes.
3. Develop operational profiles such as workload characterization of peak, prime and off hours.
4. Prepare tools and procedures for testing according to the test plan.
5. Execute system tests.
6. Interpret failure data using tools such as Pareto charts, M-tests and software reliability models.

Software reliability estimation and tracking can be part of an overall metrics program. Chapter 4 described such programs in detail. In conclusion, we will revisit the Hitachi case study in order to present their approach to reliability estimation and tracking which has become a benchmark for software developers.

6.6 THE HITACHI SOFTWARE ENGINEERING CASE STUDY REVISITED

Software development projects at Hitachi (see [1]) are managed using a Quality Progress Diagram (QPD). The QPD tracks two important numbers. The first is the target number of Program Checking Lists (PCL) to be tested each day. This information is presented on a curve that shows how many PCLs remain untested by the end of each day. The second number is a forecast of the number of expected faults. This information is used to draw a second curve tracking cumulative number of expected and actual number of faults.

The number of Program Checking Lists to be tested, each day, and the cumulative number of expected faults are determined on the basis of basic data such as:

- Program size
- Program functionality (operating system, data base, on-line)
- Previous fault record of the program (in case of enhancements)
- Development environments and available tools

- Language used
- Development type (new or reused)
- Fault record of similar projects
- Programmer experience and expertise

The Quality Progress Diagram consists of three superimposed curves:

1. Actual and target numbers of untested Program Checking Lists
2. Actual and expected cumulative number of faults
3. Backlog of faults

Tracking these curves provides a balanced view of the testing and development efforts progress and quality. Deviations can be caused by poorly planned or executed Program Checking Lists and an unusual number of faults—either too high or too low.

Hitachi is reporting an impressive record of quality and productivity improvements. Figure 6.3 shows the significant decrease in software systems failure rates over a 12 year period and Figure 6.4 shows the distribution of faults by stages in the life cycle where they are detected. Only 0.02% of the failures are reported by customers.

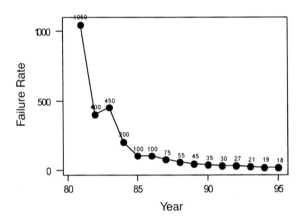

Figure 6.3 Number of Hitachi system failures, per month, per 1000 systems (over 12 years).

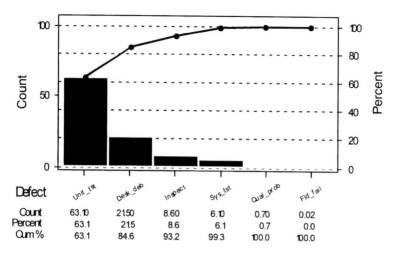

Defect	Unit_tst	Desk_deb	Inspect	Sys_tst	Qual_prob	Fld_fail
Count	63.10	21.50	8.60	6.10	0.70	0.02
Percent	63.1	21.5	8.6	6.1	0.7	0.0
Cum%	63.1	84.6	93.2	99.3	100.0	100.0

Figure 6.4 Pareto chart of faults by stages in the Hitachi life cycle.

The complete data is:

- Unit testing: 63.1%
- Desk debugging: 21.5%
- Inspections: 8.6%
- Quality probes: 0.7%
- Field failures: 0.02%

Most failures at Hitachi are identified and fixed before system test. Since failures detected by customers are much more expensive than failures detected in early stages of development, Hitachi's performance is demonstrating a winning combination—high quality at low cost! A case study from the telecommunication industry with similar results can be found in Kenett and Koenig [16] and Kenett [17]. The chapters in [18] include additional case studies from AT&T, Westinghouse and IBM.

6.7 SUMMARY

Chapter 6 focused on the analysis of data collected during dynamic testing of software systems. The chapter began with an introduction to software testing emphasizing the need for test planning. A section on definitions of software reliability terms set the background for an extensive section on software reliability models. Several models were presented, with examples. A special section on data domain models using statistically designed testing experiments concluded that section and provided new directions for researchers and practitioners to investigate. Throughout the chapter a case study from Hitachi Software was used to demonstrate how data is used efficiently and effectively by an organization that singled out the reliability of its software products as a critical success factor.

REFERENCES

1. Onoma, A. and Yamura, T. "Practical Steps Toward Quality Development," *IEEE Software*, pp. 68–76, September 1995.
2. ANSI/IEEE Std. 729-1983. *IEEE Standard Glossary of Software Engineering Terminology*, IEEE Standards Office, P.O. Box 1331, Piscataway, NJ, 1983.
3. MIL-STD-1679(Navy). *Military Standard Weapon System Software Development*, Department of Defense, Washington, D.C. 20360, December 1, 1978.
4. Wood, A. "Predicting Software Reliability," *IEEE Software*, pp. 69–77, November 1996.
5. Moranda, P. and Jelinski, Z. *Final Report on Software Reliability Study, McDonnell Douglas Astronautics Company*, MDC Report No. 63921, 1972.
6. Littlewood, B. and Verall, B., "A Bayesian Reliability Growth Model for Computer Software," *The Journal of the Royal Statistical Society*, Series C, 22, 3, pp. 332–346, 1973.
7. Musa, J., Iannino, A., and Okumuto, K. *Software Reliability Measurement, Prediction, Application*, McGraw-Hill, New York, 1987.
8. Lipow, M. "Models for Software Reliability," Proceedings of the Winter Meetings of the Aerospace Division of the American Society for Mechanical Engineers, 78-WA/Aero-18, pp. 1–11, 1978.
9. Neufelder, A. *Ensuring Software Reliability*, Marcel Dekker, 1993
10. Kenett, R. S. and Pollak, M. "A Semi-Parametric Approach to Testing For Reliability Growth, with Application to Software Systems," *IEEE Transactions on Reliability*, pp. 304–311, August 1986.
11. Kenett, R. S. and Pollak, M. "Data-analytic Aspects of the Shiryayev-Roberts Control Chart: Surveillance of a Non-homogeneous Poisson Process." *Journal of Applied Statistics*, Vol. 23, No. 1, pp. 125–127, 1996.
12. Wall, J.K. and Ferguson, P.A. "Pragmatic Software Reliability Predic-

tion," Proceedings of the Annual Reliability and Maintainability Symposium, pp. 485–488, 1977.

13. Kenett, R. S. and Zacks, S. *Modern Industrial Statistics: Design and Control of Quality and Reliability*, Dunbury Press, 1998.

14. Brown, J.R. and Lipow, M. "Testing for Software Reliability," Proceedings of the International Conference on Reliable Software, IEEE, 1975.

15. Nelson, E. "Estimating Software Reliability from Test Data," *Microelectronics and Reliability*, 17, pp. 67–73, 1978.

16. Kenett, R. S. and Koenig S. "A Process Management Approach to Software Quality Assurance," *Quality Progress*, pp. 66–70, November 1988.

17. Kenett, R. S. "Managing a Continuous Improvement of the Software Development Process," Proc. of the 8th IMPRO Conference, Atlanta, 1989.

18. Kenett, R. S. "Understanding the Software Process" in *Total Quality in Software Development*, Schulmeyer, G. and McManus, J., eds. Van Nostrand Reinholt, 1992.

19. Kanoun, K., Kaaniche, M., and Laprie, J-C. "Qualitative and Quantitative Reliability Assessment," IEEE Software, pp. 77–87, April 1997.

20. Tartalja, I. and Milutinovic, V. "Classifying Software-Based Cache Coherence Solutions," IEEE Software, pp. 90–101, June 1997.

21. Binder, R.W. "Modal Testing Strategies for OO Software," IEEE Computer, pp. 97–99, November 1996.

7
Software Review and Inspection Processes

This chapter deals with methods to plan and improve software inspection processes. In particular, it will show how to assess the effectiveness of software inspections, walkthroughs, and design reviews from data collected from the preparation and conduct of such reviews. We begin with an introduction to software inspection processes. Basic tools for the analysis of defect data are presented, followed by a statistical tool used in this context. Special attention is given to the Software Trouble Assessment Matrix (STAM) that can be used to evaluate the effectiveness of inspection processes. The chapter concludes with a section on planning and controlling software inspections.

7.1 INTRODUCTION TO SOFTWARE REVIEWS

In order to reduce the number of delivered errors or faults in software it is estimated that most companies spend between 40–50 percent of their software development efforts on testing [1]. This results from insufficient emphasis on detection and removal of errors during the earlier phases of the development effort, and what sometimes appears to be a last gasp, heroic effort to find the errors before the software goes out the door. Based on studies by Boehm [2], the cost of error removal at that point in the development effort is considerably higher than in the earlier stages. For example, the cost of fixing a requirements-related error after the software has reached production status is approximately 100 times greater than it would have been were it detected during requirements analysis. Thus, reducing the efforts on testing is a key issue in attaining higher productivity and lower cost in software development.

Generally, software reviews are considered to be one of most effective techniques for reducing testing efforts. Such reviews are implemented in the form of design reviews, code reviews, inspections, and walkthroughs. Software reviews can be classified into two types: management reviews and technical reviews. Management reviews consist of an evaluation of a project level plan or project status relative to that plan. Technical reviews are an evaluation of software elements by a team of designers and programmers. We distinguish between two types of technical reviews: walkthroughs and inspections. Section 7.2 focuses on management reviews, Section 7.3 elaborates on the planning and conduct of software walkthroughs and software inspections.

7.2 MANAGEMENT REVIEWS

The IEEE 730.1-1989 standard on Software Quality Planning [3] stipulates that a minimum of eight types of reviews are to be conducted:

1. Software Requirements Review (SRR)
2. Preliminary Design Review (PDR)
3. Critical Design Review (CDR)
4. Software Verification Review
5. Functional Audit
6. Physical Audit
7. In-Process Audit
8. Managerial Reviews

These audits and reviews implicitly delineate several subprocesses and their expected "outputs." A separate section of the IEEE standard deals with "Problem Reporting and Corrective Action," indicating how feedback is provided to resolve problems and improve these subprocesses.

The U.S. Department of Defense (DoD) has long recognized the importance of such reviews. These have been implemented on defense contracts for quite a number of years, and have been applied to systems independent of whether or not they contained software.

DoD-STD-2167A [4] defined explicit requirements for management reviews for software. The standard states:

> The software development process shall include the following major activities, which may overlap and may be applied recursively or in an iterative manner:
>
> a. System Requirements Analysis/Design
> b. Software Requirements Analysis
> c. Preliminary Design
> d. Detailed Design
> e. Coding and Computer Software Unit Testing
> f. Computer Software Component Integration and Testing
> g. Computer Software Configuration Item Testing
> h. System Integration and Testing

Moreover "During the software development process, the contractor shall conduct or support formal reviews and audits as required by the contract." Again, several subprocesses are identified and compliance with the standard requires a formal mechanism for reviewing the outputs of these subprocesses. The specific criteria for how the reviews were to be organized were specified in MIL-STD-1521B [5]. This standard defined criteria for the conduct of the meetings, as well as the materials to be reviewed at each type of review.

DoD-STD-2167A has been replaced by MIL-STD-498 [6], which is soon to be replaced by the ANSI/IEEE/EIA version of ISO Standard 12207 [7]. The U.S. version of 12207 will be a commercial standard, incorporating some of the features of MIL-STD-498, thus permitting the DoD to let software development contracts imposing requirements on the contractor to use best commercial practices. Neither of these standards invoke formal reviews. These are left to the contractor's discretion, or, conversely, the Government Program Office can require these reviews in the Statement Of Work. MIL-STD-498 specifically states that the contractor proposes the reviews to be held, with the approval of the Program Office. An appendix to MIL-STD-498 identifies a number of candidate reviews, and the contractor is free to pick and choose from these for the proposed reviews.

This change in philosophy is a result of complaints about the formal reviews being a de facto imposition of the waterfall development model. Many contractors also felt that in-process reviews, such as inspections and walkthroughs, provided more useful information, and didn't require as much cost and effort for both preparation for and conduct of the meetings. It was felt by many that the reviews were enormous "dog and pony shows," with much preparation of briefing materials, little substance, and tasty refreshments. It is our experience that these reviews, held properly, provide much useful information. While in-process reviews are extremely important, it is also important, at key milestones, to step back and look at the big picture. For instance, detailed design walkthroughs or inspections provide excellent opportunities for catching logic errors and requirements noncompliances early; however, a formalized review of the entire detailed design enables the affected parties to look at the big picture and verify that the software interacts together properly and satisfies the requirements in the main.

7.3 SOFTWARE WALKTHROUGHS AND SOFTWARE INSPECTIONS

The sole objective of technical reviews of software is to uncover errors. Such reviews may be performed at the conclusion of each of the phases of the software development life cycle. In this way, errors are prevented from infiltrating to following phases of the life cycle, in which the cost of correcting these same errors will be much grater. The success of technical reviews is measured by the percentage of errors discovered in them. These reviews take advantage of the effects of the group dynamic of teamwork, as additional leverage for discovering larger quantities of errors than would be discovered by the same team members working as isolated individuals.

7.3.1 Software Walkthroughs

A walkthrough is a review method in which a designer or programmer leads members of the development team and other interested parties through requirements, a segment of documentation, design, or code, and the participants ask questions and make comments about possible errors, violation of development standards and other problems. A characteristic of walkthroughs is that all review members, except for the designer and programmer, do not have to understand the details (structure, algorithm, data structure, etc.) of all products in advance.

Walkthroughs are typically conducted according to the following rules:

1. They are arranged and scheduled by the developer of the work product being reviewed. Sometimes, they may be arranged for and scheduled by the project lead.
2. The project schedule allocates time for walkthroughs to be held.
3. Management does not ordinarily attend the walkthrough.
4. The developer selects the list of reviewers, which is reviewed and approved by management, to ensure participation of developers of related products. Participants can include designers of the system, documentors of the function being reviewed, testers responsible for functional and system testing, developers of other parts of the system and developers of interfacing systems. Sometimes, developers from other projects will be invited as participants in order to get an independent perspective, unbiased by knowledge of the project's unique characteristics.
5. Reviewers are given the materials in advance of the meeting, typically three days to one week before the walkthrough session, and are expected to review them ahead of time and come prepared with a list of questions.
6. Typical walkthroughs are scheduled to last for no more than two hours. If the materials have not been completely reviewed at the end of that period, or if a significant list of issues has been created, another walkthrough is scheduled.
7. One person is appointed to guide the session. This person should be trained to perform that role. That person compiles an action list consisting of all errors, discrepancies, exposures, and inconsistencies uncovered during the walkthrough.
8. All issues are resolved after the session. The walkthrough provides problem detection, not problem resolution.
9. The results may or may not be reported. Some organizations prefer to leave it to the walkthrough participants to ensure that the problems are resolved. Other organiza-

tions, at minimum, prefer to capture error data for use in process improvement activities.

7.3.2 Software Inspections

Inspection is another review method that relies on visual examination of development products to detect errors, violation of development standards and other problems. Inspections provide a more formal and rigorous method of performing technical reviews at the end of development phases of the life cycle. Software inspections follow the following rules:

1. Inspections appear as separate schedules activities in the project development plan, and the work schedule contains a time allowance for rework of deficiencies identified in the inspection process.
2. Each development phase, at the end of which work products are to be inspected, is defined. Exit criteria are also defined.
3. At the end of an inspection, formal approval is required that deficiencies have been satisfactorily reworked and exit criteria have been satisfied, before work can proceed to the next development phase.
4. A specially trained moderator schedules and conducts the inspections on the basis of special skills of knowledge. The moderator is not the developer of the product being inspected nor a member of the development team; he does not usually devote full time to this role, but is a working analyst of programmer. A moderator's work may be inspected in turn by inspectors from other projects.
5. The inspection of a work product at the end of a development phase consists of six well defined steps:
   a. Planning, during which the moderator schedules inspection activities and makes sure that inspection materials have been distributed.
   b. Overview, presented by the author of the materials to those who are to participate in the inspections.
   c. Preparation, during which the participants study the materials.

    d. Inspection meeting, during which the participants concentrate on finding errors in the material.

    e. Rework, wherein the author corrects the errors found in the meeting and summarized and reported by the moderator.

    f. Follow up, during which the moderator certifies the author's rework and authorizes the next development phase, and during which data is analyzed.

The inspection technique emphasizes the accumulation and analysis of data about the types of errors and their frequency. As the data base of error patterns grows larger and the moderators gain experience with error detection, the moderator can better analyze the results of inspections, can better help designers and implementers avoid errors, and can help inspection teams learn to do a more thorough job of error detection. Checklists developed from the data base assist in this by assuring that all reasonable questions have been considered during an inspection. Also, by comparing current inspection results against the data base, both developers and management can become aware of situations in which corrective action must be taken to avoid schedule delays or to reduce the likelihood of creating excessively error-prone units of software. Accumulation and analysis of error patterns can also highlight for management those development practices in need of revision or suggest some that could be initiated, thus leading to an improved development process.

7.3.3 Differences Between Walkthroughs and Inspection

Key differences exist between walkthroughs and inspections. They may be characterized as follows:

1. Walkthroughs are informal. In some case, the developer may request them, and in others, they may be a scheduled activity, with the specific date to be decided by the developer or his supervisor. They may be performed on completed activities or during the development of an activity.

2. Walkthroughs, unlike inspections, do not require formal approval although a second walkthrough is usually performed when a "large" number of errors has been detected.

3. The moderator of an inspection is not part of the team that developed the work product. He is trained in the skills required for the moderator's role: Planning the inspections, selecting the participants, preparing for the inspection meeting, maintaining an efficient pace during the inspection meeting, assuring that all reasonable error possibilities have been considered, keeping interpersonal friction to a constructive level, recording and categorizing errors, following up on rework, and analyzing inspection results. He carries the experience he gains from project to project and becomes an expert in making the most effective possible use of the participant's time.

4. The inspection is divided into six distinct steps, each of which has its own stated objectives. In walkthroughs, these steps exist but are blended together, with several objectives being addressed simultaneously.

5. At a walkthrough meeting the developer of the work product usually conducts the meeting and "reads" the materials. At inspections, the moderator conducts the meeting and designates someone other than the developer to read the materials, so that the developer's interpretation can not inadvertently cover up errors.

6. Errors detected during the preparation period and discussed with the developer are usually not brought up at a walkthrough meeting. During inspection meetings, all errors are noted and described to establish error patterns, improve the skills of all the participants, and flag any schedule slippage as early as possible.

7. Management does not attend walkthroughs because their presence may interfere with the free flow of discussion among the working group members. Managers are not discouraged from attending inspections but usually cannot add valuable inputs to an essentially technical discussion. Management, however, is always informed of the results of inspection meetings, including data such as lines of code completed, error rates, and time expected for rework and retesting.

In summary, walkthroughs rely heavily on technical team self control and tends to confine the visibility of shortcomings to within the development team itself. On the other hand, the inspection process allows for such visibility to extend beyond the development team and imposes technical controls from sources that are external to the team.

Checklists and checksheets are sometimes used in walk-throughs and almost always used in inspections. The next sections discuss how these tools used and how data collected in the process is analyzed.

7.4 BASIC ANALYSIS OF SOFTWARE DEFECTS

7.4.1 Checklists and Checksheets

Documents and code are reviewed before, during, or after testing. In order to facilitate such reviews, *checklists* that consist of specific questions are used. Checklists provide a structure to inspections, reviews, and walkthroughs. Such lists can be improved with time and accumulated experience. *Checksheets* are used to record information gathered in tests and reviews. A sample code walkthrough checklist and a related checksheet are presented below. The checklist items are classified, during a review, as being satisfied (Yes), not satisfied (No), or not applicable (N/A). When not satisfied the noncompliance is classified as major or minor, and then as missing (M), wrong (W) or extra (E).

Code Walkthrough Checklist

Module ID: _____ Walkthrough number: _____

Walkthrough performed by: _____

Date: _____ Reinspection required? _____ (Y/N)

Walkthrough checklist	Yes	No	N/A
Programming engineering Does the code match the detailed design?			
Is the object/class breakdown logical?			
Is the data transfer between the modules correct?			
Does each class output only necessary routines and variables?			

Walkthrough checklist	Yes	No	N/A
Are the class description headers complete and updated?			
Were the coding rules observed?			
Is the code written clearly?			
Is the code efficient?			
Is the code platform independent?			
Is the code maintainable?			
Does the code contain all the necessary standard tests?			
Is the recovery from faults satisfactory?			
Is there good use of existing code?			
Can the code be reused?			
Variables Are the variables initiated prior to use?			
Are the variables with unique names?			
Are the arrays' indices within the correct ranges?			
Is the access to multidimensional arrays correct?			
Does the access to the pointers relate to defined memory area?			
Are the different accesses to the same memory area correct?			
Are the fixed values correct?			
Are the border cases of loops and indexes correct?			
Is there any access to free memory space?			
Are all the names meaningful?			
Calculation Are the types in the calculation correct?			
Is the possibility of overflow or underflow checked?			
Is the possibility of division by 0 checked?			
Are the components of a logical Boolean expression?			
Are the preferences and brackets order correct?			

Walkthrough checklist	Yes	No	N/A
If there is a macro in calculation—are there proper brackets?			
Control Are the case sections taking care of all cases?			
Does each loop have end conditions?			
Does each program have exit treatment?			
Does the program have a relevant exit value?			
Are all code sections accessible?			
Are the loop variables initialized and checked correctly?			
Are the exit conditions of the loop correct?			
Interfaces Is the call to routines compatible to their definitions?			
Are trace messages—system/process inserted?			
Are constants transferred to routines expecting variables?			
Does the function return the defined value?			
Input / Output Is the call to the routines correct (open, read, close)?			
Are EOF, EOLINE being checked?			
Is there any handling with inputs/outputs error?			
Is the divider for reading large enough?			
Is a temporary file name unique?			
Does a file close after an error occurs?			
Miscellaneous Were the compilation mistakes corrected?			
Do debug code or old notes remain?			
Are warnings analyzed?			

The following code walkthrough checksheet is used to consolidate the review's findings. The form is completed from the checksheet by aggregating the noncomplying cases, by classification items.

<u>Code Walkthrough Checksheet</u>

Module ID: _____ Walkthrough number: _____

Walkthrough performed by: _____

Date: _____   Reinspection required? _____ (Y/N)

M: Missing W: Wrong E: Extra	Major			Minor			Total	Percent
	M	W	E	M	W	E		
Programming engineering								
Variables								
Calculations								
Control								
Interfaces								
Input/output								
Miscellaneous								
Total								100%

7.4.2 Pareto Chart Analysis

When observing events, it is a universal phenomenon that approximately 80% of events are due to 20% of the possible causes. Examples include distribution of income of a firm where 20% of the clients generate 80% of the revenues, personnel management where a few employees account for the majority of absences, and typical meetings, where a few people tend to make the majority of comments, while most people are relatively quiet. A classical application to software is the general fact that 80% of software failures can be attributed to 20% of the code. This universal observation was first made by Joseph M. Juran who, in the early 1950s, coined the term "Pareto Principle" which leads to the distinction between the "vital few" and the "useful many" (Kenett [8]). The Pareto principle is so obvious and so simple that one might wonder where its added value is. Price [9] eloquently describes its power by specifying that

> it signals those targets likely to yield maximum results by the deployment of limited effort. In acknowledging that there is little point in frittering away resources through fighting where the battle isn't raging, it pinpoints the most vulnerable areas of the enemy's line, so to speak. It is a technique which finds profitable employment when you are required to sort out a messy quality control situation. When customer's rejections are bombarding you so thick and so fast that you don't know where to begin, Pareto tells you.

The Pareto Chart is a graphical display of the Pareto Principle. It consists of bar graphs sorted in descending order of the relative frequency of errors by category. Pareto charts are used to choose the starting point for problem solving, monitor changes, or identify the basic cause of a problem.

An interesting example of a Pareto Chart analysis is provided by data from Knuth [10] on changes made during a period of ten years, in the development of TEX, a software system for typesetting. Knuth's log book contains 516 items for the 1978 version, which is labeled TEX78, and 346 items for the 1982 version, labeled TEX82. These entries are classified into 15 categories ($K = 15$). The fifteen categories are:

A—Algorithm: A wrong procedure has been implemented.
B—Blunder: A mistaken but syntactically correct instruction.
C—Cleanup: An improvement in consistency or clarity.
D—Data: A data structure debacle.
E—Efficiency: A change for improved code performance
F—Forgotten: A forgotten or incomplete function.
G—Generalization: An change to permit future growth and extensions.
 I—Interaction: An change in user interface to better respond to user needs.
L—Language: A misunderstanding of the programming language.
M—Mismatch: A module's interface error.
P—Portability: A change to promote portability and maintenance.

Q—Quality: An improvement to better meet user requirements.

R—Robustness: A change to include sanity checks of inputs.

S—Surprise: Changes resulting from unforeseen interactions.

T—Typo: Change to correct differences between pseudo-code
and code.

The A, B, D, F, L, M, R, S, and T classifications represent development errors. The C, E, G, I, P, and Q classifications represent "enhancements," consisting of unanticipated features that had to be
added in late development phases. These enhancements indicate a
lack of understanding of customer requirements, and, as such, can
be considered failures of the requirements analysis process.

Figure 7.1 presents a Pareto chart of the TEX78 data. The chart
does not show any dominant error category so that, apparently, the
Pareto Principle does not apply to this data. Figure 7.2 is the Pareto
chart of the TEX82 data. Here we notice that categories C, R, G, I,
and E contribute 71% of the errors. Categories C, G, I, and E being
classified as "enhancements" which are therefore the main cause behind the logbook entries.

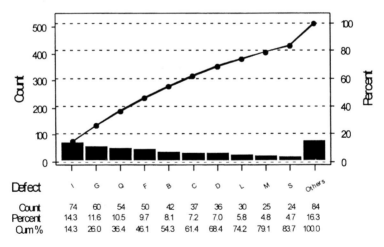

Figure 7.1 Pareto chart of TEX78 logbook data.

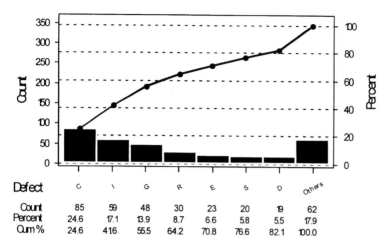

Defect	C	\	G	R	E	S	D	Others
Count	85	59	48	30	23	20	19	62
Percent	24.6	17.1	13.9	8.7	6.6	5.8	5.5	17.9
Cum %	24.6	41.6	55.5	64.2	70.8	76.6	82.1	100.0

Figure 7.2   Pareto chart of TEX82 logbook data.

7.4.3   The M-Test

Suppose we wish to compare two similar Pareto charts, containing similar categories of data, but the data were captured during two separate time intervals. A reason we might want to do this comparison is to see if there have been any significant changes that occurred between these two intervals. Figures 7.1 and 7.2 present two Pareto charts that we might want to compare. We will now describe a statistical technique specifically designed to perform such comparisons for any type of Pareto chart, whether the Pareto principle applies or not.

The M-test enables us to compare a given Pareto chart to a previously established "standard" Pareto chart with the same categories. Assume the chart we want to compare to a standard Pareto chart is based on a total of N observations subdivided into K categories, with n_i observations in category i. Let p_i be the expected proportion of observations in category i, according to the standard Pareto chart.
The M-test consists of five steps:

1. Compute the expected number of observations in category i, $E_i = N_{pi}$, i = 1, . . . K.
2. Compute $S_i = SQRT[N_{pi}(1-p_i)]$, i = 1, . . . K.

3. Compute the adjusted residuals $Z_i = (n_i - E_i)/S_i$, $i = 1, \ldots$ K.

4. For a given value of K and a 10%, 5% or 1% significance level determine the critical value C of Z_i from Table 7.1:

Table 7.1 Critical Values for M-test

K: number of categories	Significance level		
	10%	5%	1%
4	1.95	2.24	2.81
5	2.05	2.32	2.88
6	2.12	2.39	2.93
7	2.18	2.44	2.99
8	2.23	2.49	3.04
9	2.28	2.53	3.07
10	2.32	2.57	3.10
20	2.57	2.81	3.30
30	2.71	2.94	3.46

5. If all adjusted residuals, Z_i, are smaller, in absolute value, than C, no significant changes in Pareto charts are declared. Cells with values of Z_i, above C or below $-C$ are declared significantly different from the corresponding cells in the standard Pareto chart.

We now revisit Knuth's data by taking the 516 reported errors in TEX78 as a "standard" against which the 346 errors in TEX82 are measured provides another opportunity to use the M-test. In this example we will keep the categories by alphabetical order so as to facilitate the comparison between TEX78 and TEX82.

Table 7.2 M-test Applied to Knuth's Data

Category	TEX78	P_i	TEX82	E_i	S_i	Z_i
A	23	0.04	14	15.42	3.84	−0.37
B*	42	0.08	7	28.16	5.09	−4.16*
C*	37	0.07	85	24.81	4.80	12.54*
D	36	0.07	19	24.14	4.74	−1.08
E*	17	0.03	23	11.40	3.32	3.49*
F*	50	0.10	13	33.53	5.50	−3.73*
G	60	0.12	48	40.23	5.96	1.30
I	74	0.14	59	49.62	6.52	1.44

For Knuth's data K = 15 and for a significance level of 1%, one derives by interpolation in the M-test table that C = 3.20. Table 7.2 presents the various data and computations necessary to perform the M-test. A star indicates a significant difference at the 1% level. Figure 7.3 presents the proportions of errors in TEX 78 (P_i), by category and Figure 7.4 shows the difference between the TEX82 actual data and what was expected to happen with 346 errors following the same distribution as that of TEX78 (Ei). Figure 7.5 is a bar chart of the standardized residuals, Z_i. Values above 3.2 and below -3.2 indicate differences between TEX78 and TEX82 which are significant at the 1% level. TEX82 contains significantly *more* errors in the cleanup (C), efficiency (E), and robustness (R) categories than TEX78. Significantly *fewer* errors are found in blunder (B), forgotten (F), language (L), mismatch (M), and quality (Q). Knuth gives us

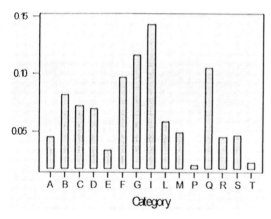

Figure 7.3 Distribution of proportion of software errors in TEX78.

Table 7.2 (Continued)

Category	TEX78	P_i	TEX82	E_i	S_i	Z_i
L*	30	0.06	2	21.12	4.35	-4.16*
M*	25	0.05	0	16.76	3.99	-4.20*
P	10	0.02	12	6.71	2.56	2.06
Q*	54	0.10	14	36.21	5.69	-3.90*
R*	23	0.04	30	15.42	3.84	3.80*
S	24	0.05	20	16.09	3.92	1.00
T	11	0.02	0	7.38	2.69	-2.75

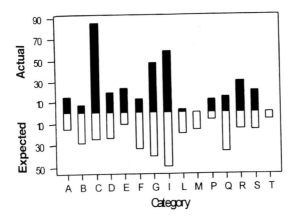

Figure 7.4 Actual (black) and expected (white) software errors in TEX82 based on N = 346 and TEX78 proportions.

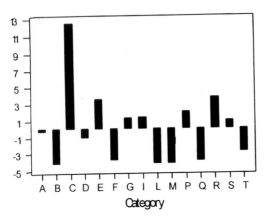

Figure 7.5 Standardized residuals for software errors in TEX82. Values above 3.2 (actuals higher than expected) and, below −3.2 (actuals lower than expected) are significant at the 1% level.

only clues as to the possible reasons for these differences. (For additional case studies and more on statistical methods used to compare Pareto charts, see Kenett [8,11,12]).

Investigating differences between Pareto charts complements the analysis of overall process error levels and trends. Increases or decreases in such error levels may result from changes across all error categories which will not show up in a Pareto chart. On the other hand, there may be no changes in error levels but significant changes in the mix of errors across categories.

7.5 LIMITATIONS OF THE SOFTWARE INSPECTION PROCESSES

In planning software inspections one should weigh costs and benefits. Such considerations must account for limitations of the software inspection process. In particular, it is not the case that more inspections with many people attending always provide the expected benefits. In this section, we review limitations of inspection processes as ascertained in empirical studies.

Inspection costs involved can be subdivided into three categories that match the main steps of an inspection process. The steps are:

1. Individual analysis
2. Team analysis
3. Repair

The costs and benefits of this process are driven by several mechanisms:

- Inspection process structure specifying, in detail, the inspection process
- Techniques used in the inspection process
- Reviewer's ability
- Code and document's quality
- Interaction with other inspections, project schedule, and personal workloads
- Tools and infrastructure

Inspection processes can use various methods such as Fagan inspections, active design reviews, phased inspections, and two-person interactions. The main differences between these methods involve the size of the review team, the number of teams, and the strategy to coordinate multiple teams. Various experiments performed at Lucent Technologies and the University of Maryland indicated that the structure of the inspection process alone does not affect the inspection effectiveness [13,14]. It was shown that the code size and functionality, together with the reviewer's ability, determine to a great extent the effectiveness of inspections—far more than the inspection structure.

Because meetings are expensive, it is important to determine exactly how they contribute to inspections and whether superior alternatives exist. Meetings can be effective if many of the existing faults are found as a result of the meeting.

In planning inspections one can consider three approaches to inspecting software:

1. Team with individual preparation (TIP)—Individual preparation in order to become familiar with the code or document. Afterward, the team holds an inspection meeting to find faults.

2. Team with individual inspection (TII)—Individual preparation in order to detect faults. The team them meets to collect defects and, if possible, find more.

3. Individual inspection (II)—Reviewers are expected to analyze the documents individually in order to find faults. Later, each reviewer conducts a second review, again individually [16]. The intent is to maximize error detection by minimizing "losses" that could have resulted from failure to detect the error during the first review.

Organization should develop an "inspection strategy" building on inspection approaches such as TIP, TII, or II. The effectiveness of the inspection approach needs to be assessed in the context of specific organizational culture and past experience.

Experiments conducted at the University of Maryland, Lucent Technologies, and the University of Hawaii investigated the effectiveness of defect detection due to varying the following review process factors: inspection team size, single and multiple review sessions, and sessions with and without defect correction [13,14,15]. The results of these experiments showed that single reviewers were not as effective at defect detection as multiple reviewers, but, interestingly enough, that four reviewers were no more effective than two reviewers. This would imply that very small teams are more effective than larger teams. Furthermore, the findings indicated that multiple sessions (reviews) were no more effective than just a single session for the same unit of code or design.

A ground rule that is usually followed in conducting peer reviews is that the sessions focus only on error detection, and that error correction is out of scope. As noted above, these studies investigated the effect of including error correction in the review process to see if that improved the effectiveness of defect detection. It was found that this was not an effective approach since it created more disruption in the daily schedules of review attendees due to the amount of time involved in attending review meetings.

In usual practice, preparation for inspections is carried out with checklists or just intuitively. Reviewers can be assigned the general responsibility to identify as many defects as possible or specific responsibilities focusing on a limited set of issues such as ensuring appropriate use of hardware interfaces, identifying untestable requirements, or checking conformity to coding standards. Porter et al. [17] conducted a study to determine the effect of using systematic detection techniques. In this study, reviewers were assigned to use ad hoc, checklist, or scenario techniques. The scenarios were a collection of procedures for detecting particular classes of defects derived from the checklist items. Whereas the checklist items may have been a few terse statements that characterized a defect category, the scenario was a lengthier description of what the defect category involved. The results of this study showed that checklist reviewers were no more effective than ad hoc, intuitive reviewers, and that scenarios proved effective at detecting the defects that their scenarios were designed to uncover. Furthermore, scenarios did not compromise their ability in detecting other classes of defects, as well.

What emerges from these studies is a picture that demonstrates that peer reviews are effective in detecting defects, but can be performed more efficiently. Techniques are available that have the potential for improving the defect detection rate, and that require less staff hours to implement than current practice does. Should we immediately start implementing two-person review teams, utilizing scenarios? Should we continue to maintain a strict focus on error detection, and not error correction? Crawford-Hines [18] cautions that what works in one organization may be counterproductive in another. Organizational culture is an important factor influencing the process by which peer reviews are conducted. Hungerford and Hevner [19] question the extent to which the results of the studies discussed earlier [13–17] can be generalized to industry as a whole, since the studies were conducted in only one industrial setting, and two university settings. They propose further studies to explore the effect of group behavior on peer review results.

We endorse the approach set forth by Crawford-Hines [18]: use what works best in your organization's culture, and carefully pilot any improvements in the peer review process before establishing the change as a standard practice for the organization.

7.6 ASSESSING SOFTWARE INSPECTION PROCESSES WITH STAM

The Software Trouble Assessment Matrix (STAM) is a tool that software developers can use to evaluate the design and effectiveness of software inspection and testing processes so that they can be improved. STAM is used to organize relationships between three dimensions (see Kenett [20]).

Three measures are easily computed from the data collected in a STAM analysis:

- *Negligence ratio*: This ratio indicates the amount of errors that escaped through the inspection process filters. In other words, it measures inspection efficiency.
- *Evaluation ratio*: This ratio measures the delay of the inspection process in identifying errors relative to the phase in which they occurred. In other words, it measures inspection effectiveness.
- *Prevention ratio*: This ratio is an index of how early errors are detected in the development life cycle relative to the total number of reported errors. This is a combined measure of the development and inspection processes. It assesses the software developer's ability to generate and identify errors as early as possible in the development life cycle.

Process improvements are the result of attempts to learn from current and past errors. Prerequisites to such improvement efforts are that the processes have been identified and that process ownership has been established. Typical development processes consist of requirements analysis, top-level design, detailed design, coding, and testing. A causal analysis of software faults classifies faults as being attributable to errors in any one of these activities. For such an analysis to be successful, it is essential that there be agreement on the boundaries of the processes represented by these activities. In particular, the entry and exit criteria for each process have to be clarified and documented. Such definitions permit effective data collection. STAM is a method to analyze data derived by answering three questions:

- Where were errors detected in the software life cycle?
- Where were those errors actually created?
- Where could the errors have been detected?

These three dimensions are positioned like the letter T, and two check sheets are used to record the number of errors classified in the various combinations of the three dimensions. For example, consider a certain software version with a total of 110 reported errors at the completion of acceptance testing (see Table 7.3 and Figure

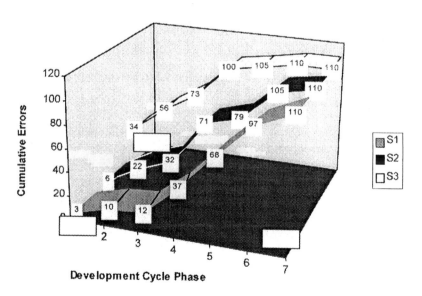

Figure 7.6 Graph of the curves determining the S1, S2, and S3 areas.

7.6). The errors were reported throughout the software life cycle, with the following distribution:

Table 7.3 Software Errors by Life Cycle Detection Phase

Life cycle phase	Number of Errors
Requirements analysis	3
Top level design	7
Detailed design	2
Programming	25
Unit tests	31
System tests	29
Acceptance test	13

From the T-type matrix in Figure 7.7, note that, of the seven errors detected during top level design, it was determined that two errors could have been detected in the review session that occurred after requirements analysis. These errors were missed by the reviewers. Of the 13 errors detected during acceptance testing, it was determined that one error could have been detected at the requirements analysis review session, one could have been detected after detailed design, six could have been detected during system testing, and five could have been detected only during acceptance testing. The implication is that eight errors escaped the inspection process filters. A similar analysis indicates that, of the five errors that could only have been detected during acceptance testing, one error is due to a requirement error, three are the result of errors in preliminary design, and one is due to a detailed design error.

A typical error analysis begins with assessing where errors could have been detected and concludes with classifying errors into the life cycle phases in which they were created. This procedure requires a repeat analysis of each recorded error. As previously mentioned, the success of an error causal analysis is highly dependent on clear entry and exit criteria for the various development phases.

Once the STAM checksheets are completed, cumulative failure profiles are drawn depicting where errors were detected, where they could have been detected, and where they were created. The areas under these three cumulative frequency curves are defined as: Sl, S2, and S3, respectively (see Figure 7.6). These areas are determined

Where were errors detected in the software life cycle?

Errors found by phase	ACCEPTANCE TEST	SYSTEM TESTS	UNIT TESTS	PROGRAMMING	DETAILED DESIGN	TOP level DESIGN	REQUITS
Requirements Analysis							8
Top Level Design						4	10
Detailed Design				1		4	5
Programming			15	15		4	5
Unit Tests			6	6		2	-
System Tests	5	5	6	6		5	5
Acceptance Tests	-	-	-	-	1	3	1
Cumulative frequency	110	110	105	100	73	56	34

CUM. CUM. FRQ. = 8, 22, 32, 71, 79, 105, 110

AREA UNDER CURVE = 8, 30, 62, 133, 212, 317, 427

	ACCEPTANCE TEST	SYSTEM TESTS	UNIT TESTS	PROGRAMMING	DETAILED DESIGN	TOP level DESIGN	REQUITS
S3	588	478	368	263	163	90	34

S2 = 427

Where could the errors have been detected?

← Errors found by phase

Where were those errors actually created?

Errors found by phase	ACCEPTANCE TEST	SYSTEM TESTS	UNIT TESTS	PROGRAMMING	DETAILED DESIGN	TOP level DESIGN	REQUITS
(totals)	14	30	31	25	2	7	3
Requirements Analysis	1	-	-	2	-	2	3
Top Level Design	-	4	1	3	1	5	3
Detailed Design	1	-	7	1	1	1	-
Programming	-	-	20	19		5	-
Unit Tests	-	5	3			2	
System Tests	6	20					
Acceptance Tests	5						
Cumulative frequency	110	97	68	37	12	10	3

	ACCEPTANCE TEST	SYSTEM TESTS	UNIT TESTS	PROGRAMMING	DETAILED DESIGN	TOP level DESIGN	REQUITS
S1	337	227	130	62	25	13	3

Figure 7.7 STAM T-matrix.

by computing the cumulative totals over the seven software development phases.

A curve is drawn by connecting the results of these additions along the seven development phases. The area under this curve, labeled S1, is approximated by adding these numbers: S1 = 3 + 10 + 12 + 37 + 68 + 97 + 110 = 337. By referring to Figure 7.7, we see that the same procedure is followed to get the S2 and S3 computations (S2 = 427 and S3 = 588).

The negligence ratio is computed using the formula: $100 \times (S2 - S1)/S1$. As previously mentioned, it measures the amount of errors that escaped through the inspection process filters, indicating inspection efficiency. High inspection efficiency corresponds to low negligence ratios. For the data in Figure 7.7, the negligence ratio is $100 \times (427 - 337)/337 = 26.7\%$, which indicates an average gap of 26.7% of a life cycle phase between actual error detection time and perfect detection under the current inspection process.

The evaluation ratio is derived using the formula: $100 \times (S3 - S2)/S2$. It measures the delay of the inspection process in identifying errors from the phase where they were created, indicating inspection effectiveness. High evaluation ratios correspond to low inspection effectiveness. For the data in Figure 7.7, the evaluation ratio is $100 \times (588 - 427)/427 = 37.7\%$, which signals the need to redesign the inspection process so that it can detect errors closer to their creation. The current inspection filters, under perfect conditions, detect errors with a delay of 37.7% of a lifecycle phase.

The prevention ratio is computed using the formula: $100 \times S1/(7 \times total)$. As previously mentioned, it indicates how early errors were detected relative to the total number of reported errors (total) in the seven development phases. If all errors were created and detected during requirements analysis, the prevention ratio would be 100%. Since early errors are less costly to correct, a high prevention ratio implies a less costly development process. Conversely, a low prevention ratio indicates that errors were detected late in the process and therefore might negatively affect delivery schedules and customer satisfaction. In Figure 7.7, the prevention ratio is 43.7%, which indicates that errors were detected late in the life cycle.

Using the negligence, evaluation, and prevention ratios, software developers can better understand and improve their inspection and development processes. They also can use STAM to benchmark different projects within their companies and against those of different companies.

REFERENCES

1. Grahm, Dorothy R. "Testing," in *Encyclopedia of Software Engineering*, Marciniak, John J., ed., New York: John Wiley & Sons, Inc., 1994.
2. Boehm, Barry W. *Software Engineering Economics*, Prentice Hall, 1981.
3. NASI/IEEE Std. 730.1-1989. *Software Quality Planning*, IEEE Standards Office, P.O. Box 1331, Piscataway, NJ, 1989.
4. DoD-STD-2167A. *Defense System Software Development*, February 29, 1988.
5. MIL-STD-1521B. *Technical Reviews and Audits for Systems, Equipments, Munitions, and Computer Programs*, June 4, 1985.
6. MIL-STD-498. *Software Development and Documentation*, December 5, 1994.
7. ISO/IEC Standard 12207. *Information Technology—Software Life Cycle Processes*, August 1, 1995.
8. Kenett, R. S. "Two Methods for Comparing Pareto Charts," *Journal of Quality Technology*, 23, pp. 27–31, 1991.
9. Price, F. *Right the First Time: Using Quality Control for Profit*, Gower Publishing Company, Brookfield, VT., 1984.
10. Knuth, D. "The Errors of TEX," Report No. STAN-CS-88-1223, Department of Computer Science, Stanford University, Stanford, CA, 1988.
11. Kenett, R. S. "Managing a Continuous Improvement of the Software Development Process," Proc. of the 8th IMPRO Conference, Atlanta, 1989.
12. Kenett, R. S. "Making Sense Out of Two Pareto Charts," *Quality Progress*, May, pp. 71–73, 1994.
13. Porter, A., Siy, H., Toman, C. and Votta, L. "An Experiment to Assess the Cost-Benefits of Code Inspections in Large Scale Software Development," *IEEE Transactions on Software Engineering*, 23(6) 1997.
14. Porter, A., Siy, H., Mockus, A. and Votta, L. "Understanding the Sources of Variation in Software Inspections," *ACM Transactions on Software Engineering Methodology,* Vol. 7, January, 1998.
15. Votta, L. "Does Every Inspection Need a Meeting?," Proceedings ACM SIGSOFT 93 Symposium on Foundations of Software Engineering, ACM, New York, 1993.

16. Porter, A. and Johnson, P. "Assessing Software Review Meetings: Results of a Comparative Analysis of Two Experimental Studies," University of Maryland, UMIACS-TR-97-15, February, 1997.

17. Porter, A., Votta, L., and Basili, V. "Comparing Detection Methods for Software Requirements Inspections: A Replicated Experiment," *IEEE Transactions on Software Engineering*, 21(6):563–575, June 1995.

18. Crawford-Hines, S. "Software Inspections and Technical Reviews: Transcending the Dogma," Fifth Annual Conference on Software Quality, ASQC, October, 1995, pp. 73–81.

19. Hungerford, B. and Hevner, A. "Team Synergy in Software Inspections," Information Systems and Decision Sciences, College of Business Administration, University of South Florida, Tampa, FL, 1997.

20. Kenett, R. S. (1996), "Assessing Sofware Development and Inspection Processes," Quality Progress, October, pp. 109–112, with correction in February, 1995.

8

Software Development Management Dashboards

8.1 INTRODUCTION

In previous chapters we presented tools and methods used by software development managers that face the major challenge of improving products and processes. This concluding chapter will integrate tools and methods implemented by several companies that decided to meet this challenge. Using a case study approach, we will systematically go from the raw data that companies collect and analyze, to the metrics they routinely report used for product and process improvements. Using real life examples, we will describe how to set up a **Software Development Management Dashboard** (SDMD). In order not to disclose any company proprietary information, we will disguise any actual companies by aggregating information from several companies and giving the company described a fictitious name. The reader will be introduced to a fictional company called MIO, Ltd. It is important to stress that MIO and the people who work at MIO do not really exist: they represent an aggregate picture that is typical of the industry. One can find many companies similar to MIO within organizations developing shrink-wrap software, embedded software, or special purpose projects (see 1,2,4).

The next section is based on observations that would typically be made during a CMM-based appraisal (see Chapter 3) at MIO, Ltd. Subsequent sections will put MIO in the context of the CMM, and then describe how MIO implemented a software process improvement program. An integral part of the software process improvement program was a metrics program leading to the development of a SDMD. We then include a section on managing a software organization with a SDMD. At the end of the chapter, we provide basic recommendations to managers who decide to personally meet the challenge of improving software products and processes in their organizations.

8.2 THE MIO CASE STUDY

8.2.1 Some Background on MIO, Ltd.

MIO develops and supplies sophisticated systems that operate on different platforms. MIO's products are distributed worldwide through local distributors with new versions coming out almost every year. Recently, MIO has been facing severe setbacks. Their new product is delayed by almost a year, and competitive pressures are building up. Traditional customers began looking at alternative products with better and more reliable performance. MIO's management decided to take a proactive role and perform an internal assessment, using the CMM as a benchmark, and a trained assessment team. This was considered a necessary first step in the deployment of the improvement plan of software products and processes.

8.2.2 Assessment Interviews at MIO, Ltd.

We join the assessment team in typical assessment discussion groups and interviews. The purpose of such interviews and discussions is to provide the assessment team with sufficient understanding about the practices in use by the software division at MIO. The information gathered by the team, the examples provided by MIO personnel, and the experience of the assessment team are used to compose the assessment findings, which will allow MIO's management to launch specific action plans.

8.2.2.1 Middle Management Discussion Group

The managers began by describing some of the tasks for which they are currently responsible. As the discussion began, one problem began to surface almost immediately: the monthly error reports that the Quality Assurance Group produced. The process is as follows:

each released MIO system accumulates and collects error conditions that occur while in use. Once a month, the errors that were recorded during the month are downloaded by MIO distributors and e-mailed to MIO headquarters for processing and reporting. The process of downloading the errors was not explained, but it is assumed to be a manual process. The files from all the sites are processed when received. Quality Assurance is responsible for overseeing this effort. This process includes the following steps:

- Data loading—In this step, error data from each system is loaded into a special purpose application developed with a 4GL application generator.
- Report generation—Once the data is loaded, error reports are generated for each MIO system version. In addition, a summary report is generated, by distributor, and for all the newly installed systems. The report formats are predefined and contain both tables and graphs.
- Interim report distribution—During the discussion, it was pointed out that certain distributors require that the generated reports be faxed to them as soon as possible, even prior to completing the statistical analysis.
- Final report distribution—When the reports are completed, they are disseminated according to a fixed distribution list that includes management and technical leaders.

There are plans to automate this process, whereby error data will automatically be collected via direct modem interfaces, requiring minimal human intervention. When the new process is implemented, the time required to produce the reports will be significantly shortened.

Another area of concern is the lack of ability to isolate and filter out errors that were recorded during scheduled maintenance or training sessions. Currently, this type of data must be identified and removed manually, which is a time-consuming process and susceptible to additional human errors.

There were several areas of deficiency related to this process that were identified during the assessment. These emerged as a consequence of the documentation reviews and the issues brought up during the discussion groups. The following are the deficiencies that were observed:

   a. There were no additional processes that analyze the errors, their source, or their cause.

   b. There was no process for tracing the errors reported and establishing their ultimate disposition and resolution. No procedures for this were found during the documentation review.

   c. There was no interface between the error reporting process and the software maintenance and software development teams. Information was thrown over the fence.

   d. There was no policy for error data retention and/or disposition, and no evidence of the existence of such a policy was found during the documentation review.

Another area of concern was staff turnover. It seemed like the company was constantly being raided by "head hunters," trying to lure away their very talented people to work for other companies. There was very little data to learn how this was affecting individual projects, in terms of how frequently this was occurring, and the types of skills being lost.

These issues were good candidates to address as part of the process improvement effort, since they currently seemed to be causing a great deal of concern in the organization.

8.2.2.2   *Requirements and Customer Interface Functional Area Representative (FAR) Discussion Group*

One of the customer representatives indicated that the ABC company, the largest client in his territory, has thirty-five MIO systems with another six on order. ABC collects statistical data on the performance of these systems. According to specifications of the MIO system, the mean time between failure (MTBF) is 5000 hours. However, in reality the MIO systems operate with an average of approximately 3000 hours MTBF. At one point in time, the MTBF was even lower. The customer representative explained how he completes problem reports after each service call, including his personal approach to investigating the problems and determining their appropriate disposition. The documentation provided with the MIO system was not always comprehensive enough, so that he made many decisions on his own. This customer representative also described how ABC was becoming more demanding with questions, such as: "What will be done by MIO in order to prevent the latest problem from reoccurring?"

Further discussion revealed that this customer representative's experience was not atypical. It was becoming evident to the assessment team that there was no clear understanding of the problems experienced by customers like ABC, and that there was no in-depth software error data recorded in the trouble report forms. In order to accomplish correction of the software, a manual preanalysis of the problem reports was required in order to isolate and classify errors resulting directly from software related problems.

8.2.2.3 *Software Design and Coding FAR Discussion Group*

Based on responses by selected participants to the CMM's Maturity Questionnaire, it was decided to formulate some open-ended questions to guide the discussion with the Software Design and Coding FAR Discussion Group. The discussion with the software design and coding FARs was to explore issues related to the software design and coding process, in particular, schedules, definition of tests, and baselines for software versions.

1. Schedules The development of schedules was very difficult for the new system version. The development team had to estimate development activities in a new environment. The lack of experience with the new development tools and the new development environment resulted in major errors in the time estimates. In addition, the FARs indicated that currently, there are no procedures or tools for collecting detailed time records by specific activities. The availability of such records could be used for developing more accurate time estimates in the future, and for comparing and reporting current plans to actual time schedules, but are not currently available.

2. Definition of tests and baselines for software versions The FARs stated that the most critical issue in releasing a new software version is the verification of the MIO system performance. This is essential for users because they must have confidence that compatibility of the MIO system is strictly enforced between software versions. A related area of concern is the integration of new software versions. There are currently no formal procedures to ensure that all the components that should be included in a particular version are indeed included. The company stated that, from what they knew, the test team is looking for ways to develop testing procedures that will cover as many conditions as possible to ensure that most (and hopefully all) bugs are detected prior to releasing a version.

A problem related to establishing a baselined reference point for performing testing is the fact that requirements keep changing. Even though there is configuration control, no one seems to be assessing the impact of the changes. Marketing, who is the customer, in effect, as far as the development group is concerned, will continuously submit changes to the requirements, even as late as the integration test cycle. Because the configuration management system operates rather slowly, the changes aren't always communicated to the developers and the testers.

These observations were confirmed by the discussion that occurred during the Test and Quality Assurance FAR Group.

These prior paragraphs are not a complete history of the discussion in these groups, nor do they represent a history of all the discussion groups. What is relevant is that these discussion groups yielded findings that later resulted in process improvement actions which were supplied by software development dashboards.

After these discussions, the assessment team members consolidated their observations and discussed (a) what they heard, and (b) what were the consequences of what they heard. The team then prepared the following preliminary findings:

- Customer problem reports are being actively collected and analyzed. This provides MIO with an opportunity to fix and follow up on customer complaints. The generated reports, however, are not used effectively and several issues with the process need to be addressed.
- Undocumented and incomplete test plans, policies, and procedures create uncertainty in the ability of MIO to properly deliver working software versions.
- Inadequate schedule and work effort estimation procedures and project plans make the planning and control of software development tasks difficult and chaotic.
- Lack of formal configuration management makes the generation of new versions a high risk operation with no management visibility of what is actually being shipped out to customers.
- The data accumulated by MIO on software products and processes is not effectively used by management.

These findings by the assessment team later resulted in a recommended process improvement project to set up the MIO-**Software Development Management Dashboard**. The MIO dashboard was designed as a graphical display of metrics measuring dimensions identified as critical to MIO by management. It is used in management and technical meetings to identify areas for improvement and track progress towards targets and goals.

These findings and action items make MIO very typical of software development organizations. The next section provides statistics derived from the SEI's database from conducted assessments that support this claim.

8.2.3 Positioning MIO in the Context of Other Software Organizations

In order to position MIO, Ltd. in the context of the capability of other software companies, we refer to the Capability Maturity Model (CMM) developed by the Software Engineering Institute (SEI). As discussed in Chapter 3, the model characterizes the capability of software development organizations, using five increasing levels of maturity and 18 Key Process Areas (see refs. 2 and 7). The higher an organization is on the maturity ladder, the greater the probability of project completion on time, with properly working products, or, in other words, the lower the development risks. To reiterate what had been described previously, the initial level is characterized by ad hoc, heroic efforts of developers working in an environment characterized by little or no project plans, schedule controls, configuration management, and quality assurance and mostly verbal undocumented communication of requirements. Going up the maturity ladder involves establishing proper project management systems, institutionalizing organization-wide practices, and establishing sound software engineering disciplines. MIO exhibits classical characteristics of a Level 1 organization.

The SEI assessment database includes findings from assessments performed in 606 organizations in recent years in a variety of companies in the U.S. and overseas (see [8]). Of these organizations, 59.4% of them (like MIO, Ltd.), are in the process of moving from the Initial Level (Level 1) to the Repeatable Level (Level 2). An additional 24.3% are in the process of moving from Level 2 to Level 3, and only 13.9% were recognized as being at Level 3.

Table 8.1 Key Process Areas by CMM Maturity Level and Activity
Domain

Level	Project management	Organization	Engineering
Optimizing		Technology change management Process change management	Defect prevention
Managed	Quantitative process management		Software quality management
Defined	Integrated software management Intergroup coordination	Organization process focus Organization process definition Training program	Software product engineering Peer reviews
Repeatable	Requirements management Project planning Project tracking and oversight Subcontract management Quality assurance Configuration management		
Initial			

Table 8.1 lists the characteristics of the 18 KPAs of the five
maturity levels with respect to their primary focus. Note that an
organization going from Level 1 to Level 2 needs to focus primarily
on establishing project management capabilities, whereas an organization going from Level 2 to Level 3 is putting in place KPAs whose
primary focus relates not only to project management concerns, but
also to establishing and institutionalizing practices for the organization as a whole. In addition, there is also focus on the practices that
affect the software engineering aspects of the software development
enterprise. Level 2 organizations, in establishing a project management discipline, are free to specify project-unique software development processes. But each project must specify a software development process, that must be documented in their project's software
development plan. Level 3 organizations, on the other hand, have
established organization-wide standard practices (which may be application domain-specific). (The CMM does encourage tailoring the

standard process for the unique characteristics of an individual project.) Establishing standardized practices represents an organization-wide concern. Similarly, the fact that a function or an organizational entity is established that has the responsibility of defining and maintaining the standard process, also represents an organization-wide concern. The KPAs which focus on software product engineering and peer reviews reflect the software engineering aspects of the organization's activities.

Organizations embarking on a metrics program in conjunction with their process improvement activities should synchronize these efforts. The focus of their metrics activities should be commensurate with the KPAs which are the focus of their process improvement efforts. The next section describes how MIO determined the appropriate metrics required to support their plan to move from the Initial Level 1 to the Repeatable Level 2.

8.2.4 Launching the MIO Metrics Program

After discussing the assessment findings, a series of process improvement action planning workshops were conducted. Based on the recommendations of the process action team, MIO's management decided to focus improvement efforts in three areas:

- Project Management
- Requirements and Configuration Management
- Quality Assurance

In order to support these efforts, a metrics program was launched. The objectives of the program were to supply the process improvement teams working in these three areas designated by management with quantitative information. These metrics are the collected and tracked on a **Software Development Management Dashboard (SDMD)**.

The metrics used in the MIO dashboard include:

Project Management—Tracking staffing—planned versus actual over time, and Software size—planned versus actual.

Requirements and Configuration Management—Requirements volatility, and tracking of requirement changes.

Quality Assurance—Problem report tracking, tracking report by severity, and software reliability estimates.

MIO is focused on one sophisticated system which is the only project undertaken by its development team. The MIO SDMD is therefore based on information from one project. Figure 8.3 presents a sample dashboard. In case the development organization is engaged in several projects simultaneously, several SDMDs will be required.

8.3 GENERIC SOFTWARE DEVELOPMENT MANAGEMENT DASHBOARDS

The Software Development Management Dashboard (SDMD) is a tool for visualizing and monitoring the status of a project. It provides information vital for predicting its future course. The charts, which are accessible to all members of the team, allow the entire project team to determine the status of a project quickly and to identify areas for improvement. The dashboard can help project managers keep their projects on course when data for the control panel is updated regularly and gauges are maintained within acceptable ranges. In general we distinguish five major categories of project data:

1. Progress reports
2. Requirements and configuration
3. Staffing levels
4. Risk analysis
5. Quality information

These categories are chosen to cover the primary areas that every project manager should track on large-scale software development projects. For each category we describe a set of generic metrics that are routinely used to manage organizations. These can, of course, be supplemented with additional metrics, as needed, to provide better insight into the status of the project.

In the next section, we present an example of a SDMD.

8.4 A SOFTWARE DEVELOPMENT MANAGEMENT DASHBOARD CASE STUDY: THE SPMN MAIN CONTROL PANEL*

In this section we describe a case study implementation of a Software Development Management Dashboard: The Control Panel developed by the Software Program Managers Network (SPMN). This SDMD is a comprehensive shareware Excel implementation that can be downloaded from www.spmn.com.

The SDMD Control Panel is a shareware tool for visualizing and monitoring the condition of a project, and predicting its future course. The panel allows the entire project team to determine the status of a project quickly, and to identify areas that need improvement. When data for the SDMD control panel is updated regularly and gauges are maintained within acceptable ranges the panel can help project managers keep their projects on schedule. The panel has five major categories and two subcategories of project data:

1. Progress
   a. Productivity
   b. Completion
2. Change
3. Staff
4. Risk
5. Quality

These categories were chosen to cover the primary areas that every project manager should track on large-scale software development projects.

The project data reported by the gauges are derived from basic data contained in an Excel workbook, which forms the basic part of the tool. It includes a spreadsheet (worksheet) of project data. That worksheet also includes a definition of project boundary conditions,

---

* We thank the Software Program Managers Network for allowing us to use the following material, which is adapted from Chapter 2, "Project Control Panel," of *The Program Manager's Guide to Software Acquisition Best Practices,* published by the Software Program Managers Network [9]. In some areas we have also amplified the descriptions.

Project Date Data				Project Baseline Data	
Type of reporting period (M = Monthly or W = Weekly)	Project start date (month/ day/year)	Total length of project (in reporting periods)	Current Reporting Period	Budget at Comple- tion (BAC)	Original number of project require- ments
Monthly	8/6/96	12	4	**10,000,000**	85

Figure 8.1   Project boundary conditions.

for example, total schedule, and budget. Figure 8.1 illustrates that portion of the spreadsheet. (The control panel which illustrates how all the information is tied together is illustrated in Figure 8.3). We will describe below how the information in the worksheet is used as input to the gauges.

The data in the original SPMN spreadsheet are color-coded. That color coding is not provided here; however, we have established a convention to map from the SPMN's color coding of the data. That convention is illustrated in Figure 8.2.

Figure 8.3 illustrates the SDMD contol panel. The gauges are numbered in the figure in accordance with their descriptors.

8.4.1   Progress

The basic data for Gauges 1, 2, 4, 5, and 6 are derived from the data contained in the portion of the spreadsheet shown in Table 8.2.

1.   The Earned Value or Budgeted Cost of Work Performed (BCWP) gauge shows the cumulative Earned Value delivered to date. The cumulative Earned Value indicator shows the amount of work that has been completed on the project. This metric is based on

Mapping to SPMN Color Code			
Reporting Period/Data	Current Reporting Period	Final Reporting Period	Data Imported from MS Project
SPMN Convention	Yellow	Red	Green
Our Convention	Normal font	*Italic font*	**Bold font**

Figure 8.2   Equivalent color-code.

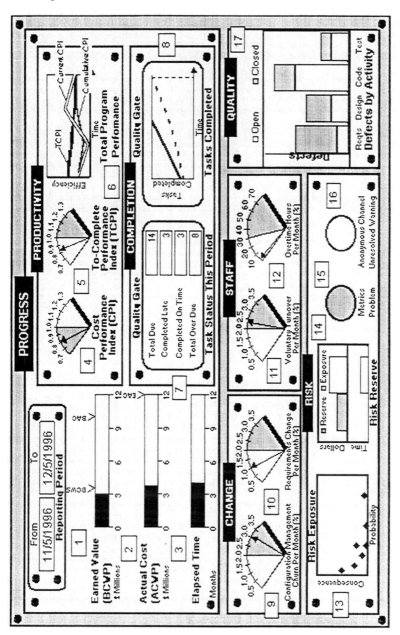

Figure 8.3   The SDMD project control panel.

Table 8.2 Cost/Schedule Performance Data

Reporting period data		Earned value measures			
Reporting period no.	Period end date	Cumulative planned value (BCWS)	Cumulative earned value (BCWP)	Actual cost (ACWP)	Estimate at completion (EAC)
1	9/5/96	500,000	500,000	650,000	10,000,000
2	10/5/96	1,000,000	970,000	1,550,000	11,000,000
3	11/5/96	2,000,000	2,000,000	2,500,000	11,500,000
4	12/5/96	3,500,000	3,000,000	3,700,000	12,000,000
5	1/5/97	4,000,000			
6	2/5/97	5,250,000			
7	3/5/97	6,150,000			
8	4/5/97	7,000,000			
9	5/5/97	7,750,000			
10	6/5/97	8,500,000			
11	7/5/97	9,250,000			
12	8/5/97	10,000,000			

the notion that, at the beginning of a project, every task is allocated a budget, which then becomes its planned value. As work is completed on a task, its budget (or planned value) is "earned" as a quantitative measure of progress. The maximum value on the gauge is the total original budget for the project known as Budget at Completion (BAC). Note that BAC is constant for the life of the project and represents the total value of work to be performed. The triangle indicator shows the cumulative planned value or Budgeted Cost of Work Scheduled (BCWS), which is the total value of work that was originally scheduled for completion by the end of this reporting period.

The cumulative earned value (BCWP), cumulative planned value (BCWS), and BAC indicators can be compared with one another to make critical observations about progress on the project. By comparing the cumulative earned value (BCWP) indicator with the cumulative planned value (BCWS) indicator, you can determine if the project is ahead of or behind schedule. This is a good measure of schedule deviation because it takes into account the amount of work that was planned to be completed.

In the example shown in Figure 8.3, it would indicate that the project is behind schedule.

Note: Establishing a planned value and a completion criterion for each task before work begins is critical for using the Earned Value metric successfully to measure progress. Cumulative Earned Value is the sum of the planned values for all completed tasks. The best completion criteria for a software task will require that no planned value credit can be taken until all work is completed and tested. These completion criteria are known as quality gates.

2. The Actual Cost or Actual Cost of Work Performed (ACWP) gauge shows the cumulative actual cost incurred on the project to date. Estimate at Completion (EAC) is the maximum value on this gauge, which represents the current best estimate for total cost of the project. Note that EAC might have a different value from BAC in the above Earned Value gauge because better total cost estimates can be made as the project progresses. Therefore EAC may change for different reporting periods.

Note: By comparing cumulative actual cost (ACWP) with the cumulative Earned Value (BWCP) in the above Earned Value gauge, you can estimate how your project is performing against its budget. This shows how well the project is turning actual costs (ACWP) into progress (BCWP). Although the scales for this gauge and the Earned Value gauge are the same, cumulative actual cost can be compared with BAC to determine project status toward overrunning the original budget, and with EAC to determine project status toward overrunning the current estimated total cost.

In the example shown in Figure 8.3, it would indicate that the project is overrunning its budget.

3. The Elapsed Time gauge shows the end date for the current reporting period.

4. The Cost Performance Index (CPI) gauge shows how efficiently the project team has turned costs into progress to date. It is calculated by dividing cumulative Earned Value by the cumulative actual cost (BCWP/ACWP). It is a historic measure of average productivity over the life of the project.

Note: CPI represents how much work was performed for each dollar spent, or "bang for the buck." When CPI has a value of 1.0, the project team is delivering a dollar of planned work for each dollar of cost. When CPI is less than 1.0, there is the potential for a productivity problem. For example, a CPI of .82 means that you got 82 cents worth of planned work for each dollar you paid in cost. A CPI of less than 1.0 may indicate that the project team didn't perform as well as expected or that the original budget was too aggressive for the amount of work to be performed.

5. The To-Complete Performance Index (TCPI) gauge shows the future projection of the average productivity needed to complete the project within an estimated budget. It is calculated by dividing the work remaining by the current estimate of remaining cost ((BAC – BCWP)/(EAC – ACWP)).

Note: The TCPI gauge must be used in conjunction with the CPI gauge. TCPI should be compared to CPI to determine how realistic the most recent estimated total cost (EAC) is for the project. Note that CPI measures the average historic productivity to date. If TCPI is greater than CPI, then the project team is anticipating an efficiency improvement to make it more productive. The estimated total cost of the project (EAC) can therefore be calibrated by comparing TCPI to CPI. Always question claims of future productivity improvement that result in a 20 percent or greater increase in TCPI over CPI in order to ensure they are based on sound reasoning. This is especially true of "silver bullets" like new tools, languages, or methodologies, which may actually decrease productivity due to training and start-up costs. The redline on this gauge should be about 20 percent above the current value of the CPI gauge to show the relationship and warning level between the two gauges.

6. The Abba* Chart, also known as a Total Program Performance Efficiency chart, is composed of four different performance indicators showing trends in historic and projected efficiency to date. The indicators are:

- TCPI (To-Complete Performance Index) (Gauge 5)
- Completion Efficiency (CE) is a ratio calculated by dividing BAC by EAC to estimate the productivity required to complete the project within a projected total cost (EAC)
- CPI Cost Perfromance Index (Gauge 4).
- Monthly CPI is a ratio calculated by dividing the monthly Earned Value by the monthly actual cost (as opposed to cumulative values for the CPI calculation).

---

* Named for Wayne Abba of the Department of Defense.

The data for the graphs are also derived from the cost/schedule data contained in the Excel workbook.

7. Quality Gate Task Status this Month shows the completion status of tasks during the current reporting period. A quality gate is a predefined completion criterion for a task. The criterion must be an objective yes/no indicator that shows a task has been completed (see discussion on Gauge 1 above). The indicators are:

- Total Due is the total number of tasks scheduled for completion during this reporting period plus any overdue tasks from previous periods. This indicates the total quantity of work required for the project to keep pace with the schedule.
- Completed Late is the number of tasks completed late during this reporting period. This number includes those tasks scheduled for this period that were completed late, as well as any overdue tasks from previous periods that were completed in this period. The Completed Late indicates how well the project is completing work, even if it is late according to the original schedule.
- Completed On Time is the number of tasks originally scheduled for completion during this reporting period that were completed by their original scheduled due date. This number indicates how well the project is keeping up with scheduled work.
- Total Overdue is the total number of tasks for all previous reporting periods that are overdue by the end of the current reporting period. This is an indicator of the quantity of work needed to get the project back on schedule.

Note: *The total number of tasks completed in this reporting period is the sum of Completed On Time and Completed Late. Total Overdue then is equal to Total Due minus Completed on Time and Completed Late.*

The data for Gauges 7 and 8 are taken from the portion of the worksheet illustrated in Table 8.3.

8. The Quality Gate Tasks Completed graph shows the cumulative number of tasks completed by the end of each reporting period to date plotted with the cumulative number of tasks scheduled for completion.

Note: *If the number of tasks completed falls below the number*

Table 8.3 Quality Gate Task Data

Reporting period data		No. scheduled this period	Total due this period (# scheduled + # overdue from last period)	No. completed on time this period	No. completed late this period	Cumulative no. overdue at end of period
Reporting period no.	Period end date					
1	9/5/96	5	5	3	1	1
2	10/5/96	7	8	2	1	5
3	11/5/96	7	12	2	2	8
4	12/5/96	6	14	3	3	8
5	1/5/97	10	18			18
6	2/5/97	12	30			30
7	3/5/97	15	45			45
8	4/5/97	13	58			58
9	5/5/97	11	69			69
10	6/5/97	16	85			85
11	7/5/97	12	97			97
12	8/5/97	5	102			102

Quality Gate Tasks

planned, then the horizontal distance on the time axis gives an idea of the current schedule slip to date.

8.4.2 Change

9. CM (Configuration Management) Churn per Month is calculated by taking the number of items under configuration control (baselined items) that have been modified and rechecked into the configuration management system over the last reporting period, and dividing it by the total number of baselined items in the system at the end of the period. It is expressed as a percentage. A modified baselined items is one that was previously in the system, but was reviewed sometime later and modified or replaced.

The worksheet data from which the CM Churn per Month for Figure 8.3 is calculated is shown in Table 8.4. It also the source for the data for Gauge 10.

Note: This gauge serves as an indicator of the architectural soundness of the system. If the rate of "churn" begins to approach the two percent per month level, this shows a lot of rework is going on,

Table 8.4 Configuration Management Data

Reporting period data		Configuration Items	
Reporting period no.	Period end date	Total no. in CM system at end of period	No. modified and rechecked into CM this period
1	9/5/96	50	1
2	10/5/96	52	0
3	11/5/96	60	3
4	12/5/96	65	2
5	1/5/97		
6	2/5/97		
7	3/5/97		
8	4/5/97		
9	5/5/97		
10	6/5/97		
11	7/5/97		
12	8/5/97		

which could point to deeper problems in the project. A high churn rate may mean that the original design was not robust enough. It could also be a symptom of changing requirements (see Gauge 10), which could indicate the project is drifting towards disaster.

10. Requirements Change Per Month is calculated by dividing the number of new, changed, or deleted requirements specified in this reporting period by the total number of requirements at the end of this period. It is expressed as a percentage. Typical projects experience a requirements change of one percent per month.

Note: Some requirements growth is to be expected, particularly on large projects. However, a high rate of requirements change can indicate the customer is not sure of what is wanted, or the original requirements definition was poor. A high rate often predicts disaster for software-intensive projects.

8.4.3 Staff

11. Voluntary Turnover per Month is calculated by dividing the number of staff leaving during this reporting period by the number of staff at the beginning of this period. It is expressed as a percentage. The target range is less than 2 percent per month. A person can leave the project in a number of ways, such as by quitting the organization or requesting reassignment to another project.

Note: Turnover is an important measure for risk assessment. Every project lasting six months or longer should expect and prepare for some staff turnover. Each project member who leaves the team causes a productivity drop and schedule disruption. Bringing on new team members, regardless of their skills and experience, does not necessarily solve the problem; they require time to become familiar with the project and processes. In addition, a productive team member will usually have to devote time to orient the new hire, thus taking away additional resources from the project. Appropriate allowances should be included in the productivity resource estimates to allow for staff turnover.

The basic data for Gauge 11 of Figure 8.3 are derived from this extract from the worksheet, and is illustrated in Table 8.5.

12. Overtime per Month is calculated by dividing the overtime hours by the base working hours for all project staff in this reporting period. It is expressed as a percentage. The target range is less than 10 percent. When the overtime rate approaches 20 per-

Table 8.5 Staffing Data

| Reporting period data | | Voluntary turnover | |
| | | No. of staff at | No. staff leaving |
Reporting period no.	Period end date	beginning of period	voluntarily this period
1	9/5/96	75	5
2	10/5/96	70	2
3	11/5/96	80	1
4	12/5/96	85	2
5	1/5/97		
6	2/5/97		
7	3/5/97		
8	4/5/97		
9	5/5/97		
10	6/5/97		
11	7/5/97		
12	8/5/97		

cent, the ability of the staff to respond effectively to crises suffers significantly.

The data for this gauge is also derived from the worksheet, and that portion of the data in the worksheet is illustrated in Table 8.6.

8.4.4 Risk

13.   The Risk Exposure chart shows each risk plotted by its cost consequence and probability. Each data point in this chart is associated with a specific risk, and would have an identifier associated with it. The probability is expressed in terms of occurrences over the life of the project. The regions on the graph show where risks fall into areas of low-, moderate-, or high-risk exposure. Clearly, high probability–high consequence risks indicate high-risk exposure, while low probability–low consequence risks indicate low-risk exposure.

Note: The SPMN has also developed another shareware program called Risk Radar [10]. Risk Radar is a risk management database, created in Microsoft Access, that helps project managers iden-

Table 8.6 Overtime Hours

| Reporting Period Data | | Overtime hours | |
| | | Base no. | No. overtime |
Reporting period no.	Period end date	staff hours this period	staff hours this period
1	9/5/96	13,000	1,000
2	10/5/96	13,500	2,000
3	11/5/96	13,500	3,375
4	12/5/96	13,200	500
5	1/5/97		
6	2/5/97		
7	3/5/97		
8	4/5/97		
9	5/5/97		
10	6/5/97		
11	7/5/97		
12	8/5/97		

tify, prioritize, and communicate project risks in a flexible and easy-to-use form. Risk Radar provides standard database functions to add and delete risks, together with specialized functions for prioritizing and retiring project risks. Each risk can have a user-defined risk management plan and a log of historical events. A set of standard short- and long-form reports and viewgraphs can be easily generated to share project risk information with all members of the development team. The number of risks in each probability / impact category by time frame can be displayed graphically, allowing the user to visualize risk priorities and easily uncover increasing levels of detail on specific risks. Risk Radar also provides flexibility in prioritizing risks through automatic sorting and risk-specific movement functions for priority ranking.

The features of the Risk Radar include:

- *A Set Up Project screen allows the project leader to set project specific information, such as the title of the project, in one place*
- *An Edit Risks Long Form screen which allows the project leader to add new risks, modify existing risks, delete risks,*

and retire risks. The screen is called a long form because it requires more than one computer screen to view it all.

- *An* Edit Risks Short Form *screen which allows the project leader to present all of the information for a risk on a single screen without scrolling. This means there is less room for field descriptions.*
- *A* View Risks *screen which is a graphical display of risks by risk exposure category and impact time frame.*
- *A* View Retired Risks *screen which provides a simple table of all risks that are no longer considered a threat, and have been retired from active risk management. This information might be useful in formulating new risks and for project postmortems.*
- *A* Prioritize Risks *screen which provides a means for prioritizing risks, using automatic sorting buttons, manually moving risks in the priority ranking, and renumbering the priority rank of all risks.*
- *A* Reports *screen which contains a set of predefined reports in both long-form (one risk per page) and short-form (one risk per line) formats that can be generated by clicking a button.*

Risk Radar data can be exported into an Excel spreadsheet. Excel spreadsheets provide the basic inputs for the control Panel. Consequently, the data from the Risk Radar can be used directly in the control Panel.

14. Risk Reserve shows the total cost risk exposure and schedule risk exposure compared to the current cost and time risk reserves for the project. Risk exposure for a risk is calculated by multiplying the probability times its potential negative consequence. Although the consequences (and therefore the risk exposure) for different risks are not necessarily independent, a first approximation to the total cost risk exposure of the project can be made by adding together the individual cost risk exposures for all risks. The same approximation to total schedule risk exposure in time can be made by adding together the individual schedule risk exposures for all risks.

The data for this gauge is also derived from the worksheet, and that portion of the data in the worksheet is illustrated in Table 8.7.

Note: Risk reserves for cost and schedule should be established at the beginning of the project to deal with unforeseen problems. The

Table 8.7 Risk Reserve Data

Reporting period data		Risk reserve	
		Total	Total
Reporting period no.	Period end date	budget risk reserve ($)	schedule risk reserve (days)
1	9/5/96	30,000	20
2	10/5/96	28,000	19
3	11/5/96	28,000	19
4	12/5/96	28,000	18
5	1/5/97		
6	2/5/97		
7	3/5/97		
8	4/5/97		
9	5/5/97		
10	6/5/97		
11	7/5/97		
12	8/5/97		

cost and time risk reserve for a project will change over time as some of these reserves are used to mitigate the effects of risks that actually occur and affect the project.

15. The Metrics Problem indicator shows that management has received either a warning or bad news about some of the metrics on the project.

16. The Anonymous Channel Unresolved Warning indicator shows that project management has received either a warning or bad news about the actual status of the project.

Note: An open-project culture in which reporting bad news is encouraged is conducive to a healthy project. Warnings from anonymous or known project personnel should be welcomed and tracked.

8.4.5 Quality

17. Defects by Activity displays the number of detected defects open (i.e., yet to be fixed) and the number of defects closed in each phase of the project. Defects are problems that, if not removed, could cause a program to fail or to produce incorrect results. Defects are

generally prioritized by severity level, with those labeled 1 being the most serious.

Note: *The quality indicators on this chart help you answer the question, "What is the quality of the product right now?"*

In the example illustrated by the control panel in Figure 8.3, the histogram depicts requirements, design, code, and test defects that have been open and closed. The raw data for the histogram is also contained in the worksheet and is illustrated in Table 8.8.

The shareware software provided by the SPMN allows the user to add or delete gauges as the user sees fit. Consequently, if there are other indicators that a project leader would like to include, they can be added. Indicators of potential use from earlier chapters are:

Pareto Chart Analysis—see Chapter 7
STAM—see Chapter 7

* Negligence ratio
* Evaluation ratio
* Prevention ratio

Number of open bugs per unit of time—see Chapter 4
Number of closed bugs—see Chapter 4
Software Specification Metrics—see Chapter 5

* Completeness
* Readability
* Accuracy
* Flesch Reading Grade Level

Predicted Failures and Failure Rates—see Chapter 6

* Jelinski-Moranda Model Estimates
* Lipow Model Estimates
* Multinomial Model Estimates
* Reliability Growth Estimates
* Data Domain Model Estimates

8.5 CHAPTER SUMMARY

Software development is an abstract activity typically carried out by individuals that work best on their own. However, successful software products require documentation, testing, quality assurance

Table 8.8   Defect Data by Activity and Category

Reporting period data		Defects by activity							
Reporting period no.	Period end date	Requirement defects open	Requirement defects closed	Design defects open	Design defects closed	Coding defects open	Coding defects open	Test defects open	Test defects closed
1	9/5/96	20	10	12	4	2	2	1	0
2	10/5/96	22	5	12	6	8	3	5	6
3	11/5/96	10	15	15	4	12	3	4	2
4	12/5/96	5	20	8	12	25	10	8	5
5	1/5/97								
6	2/5/97								
7	3/5/97								
8	4/5/97								
9	5/5/97								
10	6/5/97								
11	7/5/97								
12	8/5/97								

and proper understanding of customer requirements. This requires team work and an engineering approach to software development. MIO is still struggling in its effort to climb the maturity ladder but it has determined both a starting point and a direction. In order to improve software products and development processes, management needs *both*. Metrics and quantitative information play a crucial role in supporting improvement efforts. The MIO Software Development Management Dashboard is playing the role of a management compass. Our recommendations to software managers interested in meeting the competitive challenge are simple:

> *Find where you are,*
> *determine where you want to go,*
> *and use a compass to get there*

REFERENCES

1. Grady, R. B., (1992), *Practical Software Metrics for Project Management and Process Improvement,* Englewood Cliffs, NJ: Prentice Hall.
2. Humphrey, W. (1989), *Managing the Software Process,* New York: Addison Wesley.
3. IEEE 1044.1, (1995), Guide to IEEE Standard for Classification for Software Anomalies, IEEE Standards Department, Piscataway, NJ 08855-1331.
4. Kenett, R. S., (1989), "Managing a Continuous Improvement of the Software Development Process," *Proceedings of the Eight IMPRO Conference,* Atlanta.
5. Kenett, R. S., (1994), "Assessing Software Development and Inspection Processes," *Quality Progress,* October, pp. 109–112, with corrections in February, 1995.
6. Kenett, R. S., (1994), "Making Sense Out of Two Pareto Charts," *Quality Progress,* May, pp. 71–73.
7. Paulk, M. C., et al., (1995), *The Capability Maturity Model: Guidelines for Improving the Software Process,* New York: Addison-Wesley.
8. "Process Maturity Profile of the Software Community 1997 Update," Software Engineering Measurement and Analysis Team, Software Engineering Institute, Carnegie Mellon University, October 1997.
9. Department of Defense, Software Program Managers Network, *The Program Manager's Guide to Software Acquisition Best Practices,* April 1997.
10. Department of Defense, Software Program Managers Network, *Risk Radar User's Guide,* Version 1.1, March 1998.

Author Index

Subject Index